D0743817

From Guilt
to Glory
VOLUME II

From Guilt to Glory

VOLUME II

Reveling in God's Salvation

RAY C. STEDMAN

MULTNOMAH · PRESS

Portland, Oregon 97266

Unless otherwise identified, all Scripture references are from the Holy Bible: New International Version, copyright 1973, 1978 by the International Bible Society.

Scripture quotations marked RSV are from the Revised Standard Version of the Bible, copyright 1946, 1952, © 1971, 1973, Division of Christian Education, National Council of the Churches of Christ in the USA. Used by permission.

Scripture quotations marked KJV are from the King James Version.

Cover design by Phil Malyon and Judy Quinn
Photograph by Russ Keller

FROM GUILT TO GLORY
Volume Two
© 1978 by Ray C. Stedman
Published by Multnomah Press
Portland, Oregon 97266

Published in cooperation with Discovery Foundation,
Palo Alto, California

Printed in the United States of America

All rights reserved. No part of this publication may be reproduced, stored in a retrieval system, or transmitted, in any form or by any means, electronic, mechanical, photocopying, recording, or otherwise, without the prior written permission of the publisher.

Library of Congress Cataloging-in-Publication Data
(Revised for vol. 2)

Stedman, Ray C.
    From guilt to glory.

    "Published in cooperation with Discovery Foundation,
Palo Alto, California"—T.p. verso.
    Contents: v. 1. Hope for the helpless — v. 2. Reveling in God's salvation.
    1. Bible. N.T.—Romans—Sermons.   2. Sermons,
American.   I. Title.
BS2665.4.S73   1985   227'.1077   85-29657
ISBN 0-88080-124-2 (v. 2)

86 87 88 89 90 91 – 10 9 8 7 6 5 4 3 2 1

CONTENTS

1
HAS GOD
FAILED?

(Romans 9:1-13)

Make your way into Romans 9, and you see the apostle Paul tackling some of the toughest questions ever asked about God's actions. Here Paul faces squarely some of the most bitter accusations man has brought against God.

In the first major division of this letter, chapters 1–8, Paul explained the gospel of God's grace, the full plan of redemption. Now in the second division, chapters 9–11, he seems to be starting all over again. But this time his purpose is not to *explain* the gospel but to *exhibit* it. These three chapters are an exhibition of the grace that takes man from terrible guilt to matchless glory.

In a wax museum at San Francisco's Fishermen's Wharf you can see wax figures of famous people pictured in scenes from various historic moments. This kind of thing appeals to many, helping them grasp more clearly what those events were actually like. This is what we have in chapters 9–11 of Romans. It is a demonstration—in terms of people—of how God works in human history, how he redeems and saves.

A Sad and Sober Story

The apostle has already declared man helpless to save himself. While we have power to choose, our choices do not cover all possibilities; God's will is worked out behind it all. We do not understand this, so Paul turns the spotlight on Israel to demonstrate just how God works.

The story of Israel is sad and sobering. This nation always thought of itself as having an inside track with God. Israel was the people of God, the chosen nation, close to God, with advantages no other nation enjoyed. Yet Paul begins this section by declaring this nation to be far, far away from God. Despite the possibilities they might have enjoyed, they are a long way from doing so. Paul is not angry over this fact, nor does he come on with accusations. He begins by describing the personal anguish it causes him:

> *I speak the truth in Christ—I am not lying, my conscience confirms it in the Holy Spirit—I have great sorrow and unceasing anguish in my heart. For I could wish that I myself were cursed and cut off from Christ for the sake of my brothers, those of my own race, the people of Israel (9:1-4).*

To the Jews of his day the apostle sounded like an enemy. As he preached and taught the riches in Christ Jesus and focused on the Messiah, he became in the eyes of the Jews an enemy. This has remained true of the nation of Israel until today. They still see Paul this way. If a Jew reads the letter to the Romans, he probably regards it as a gigantic put-down to the whole nation. Paul's ministry everywhere stirred up the antagonism of the Jews.

And yet Paul is not their enemy, as he himself makes clear. He is their loving, hurting friend. To say what he does breaks his heart. The hurt is real. Paul tells us these are not crocodile tears he is shedding. This is no phony protest, like some who say, "I'm only telling you this because I love you" and then proceed to cut you to pieces. "No," Paul says, "my conscience supports me in this, and the Holy Spirit himself confirms the genuineness of my anguish. It is deep and lasting." He describes it as "great sorrow and unceasing anguish."

To Trade Places in Hell

If you love someone whose trend in life is away from Christ and the things of God, anguish and grief are always present in your heart. You may be enjoying yourself outwardly, and you may be at peace in many ways, but hurt is there like a deep knot. The moment your thoughts go back to that person you feel it again. I don't think anything is more devastating and more deeply felt than love and concern for someone drifting into destruction, danger, despair, perhaps even death, especially when you feel helpless to do anything about it. This was the apostle's position. His anguish was so deep that he says if it were possible (fortunately it wasn't) he would be willing to take their place in hell, if only they could find Christ! Such commitment is rare.

We find Moses saying something similar in Exodus 32. He came down from the mountain and found the people dancing around the golden calf, conducting themselves in riotous ways, and he intervened with God on their behalf. "Lord, if it be possible, blot this sin from their lives," he said. "But if not, blot me out of your book." That touches me. I would be willing, gladly, to give up the rest of my earthly life if it meant my loved ones would be in glory. But I can't think of anyone for whom I would give up my hope for eternity. Yet this is what the apostle feels. He knows it isn't possible, but he says, "If I could, I would."

What a lesson here on how to approach someone you want to help! If it is someone who isn't eager to receive what you have to say, you must never come on—Paul never does—with accusations, or bitter words or denunciations, or even by focusing on the issues that separate you.

Perhaps you've heard of the man who said to a friend, "I hear you dismissed your pastor. What was wrong?"

The friend answered, "Well, he kept telling us we were going to hell."

"What does the new pastor say?"

"He keeps saying we're going to hell, too."

"So what's the difference?"

"Well," the friend said, "when the first one said it, he sounded like he was glad; but when the new man says it, he sounds like it's breaking his heart." This is what Paul is saying here. To tell the Romans these things about Israel breaks his heart.

Part of the reason for this anguish is explained in what Paul says next. He recognizes the tremendous possibilities the Jews had, but failed to take advantage of.

> *Theirs is the adoption as sons; theirs the divine glory, the covenants, the receiving of the law, the*

temple worship and the promises. Theirs are the patriarchs, and from them is traced the human ancestry of Christ, who is God over all, forever praised! Amen (9:4-5).

I am reminded of a young man with whom I shared a ministry many years ago in Southern California. He had a brilliant mind, a powerful personality, keen insights into the Scriptures, and a convincing effectiveness in what he said. He is now a broken man, having drifted from the faith—an alcoholic, perhaps dying. What sorrow this brought to my heart when I heard of it, as I thought of the great possibilities now wasted.

This is how the apostle feels about the advantages Israel wasted. He lists eight of them.

First, *they were chosen as the people of God.* Scripture makes it plain God singled out this nation—the descendants of Abraham through Jacob's twelve sons—as his people. He said, "Behold, Israel is my son." He dealt with them as his specially chosen people. Gentiles have not always understood this and many times resent it. Someone has put their feeling this way:

> *How odd*
> *of God*
> *to choose*
> *the Jews!*

But God really did choose them. Their position was different from any other nation of their day, and Paul acknowledges it.

Second, *to the Jews was given the divine glory.* By this Paul means the Shekinah, the bright cloud that followed Israel through the wilderness and later abode in the Holy of Holies in the tabernacle to mark God's presence among his people. Centuries later when the temple was built by King Solomon, the cloud of glory again came and filled the Holy of Holies. The people knew God had recognized his ties with this remarkable people and was living among them. To them, indeed, "belonged the glory."

Third, *the Jews had the covenants,* those remarkable agreements God made with Abraham, Isaac, Jacob, Moses and David, in which God irrevocably committed himself to do certain things for this nation. God took the initiative to make these covenants with this strange and wonderful people.

Fourth, *the Jews had the law.* This was their dearest and greatest treasure, and still is. The book *In the Beginning* by contemporary Jewish writer Chaim Potok describes how the Jews love the Torah, the scrolls of the law. They have a service set aside in which men of the congregation take the scrolls and dance with them. Potok records how one of the young lads says to himself, "I wonder if the Goyim (Gentiles) ever feel this way about the Word of God?" Yes, the law was their greatest treasure.

Fifth, *the Jews had the temple worship.* God had carefully and meticulously described how the people should conduct themselves in his presence. He told them the kinds of offerings to bring and the ritual to carry out. He designed beautiful ways of reminding them of all he had taught them. The Jews had the temple itself, one of the most beautiful buildings ever built. It was the glory of Israel, still standing in our Lord's day and while Paul wrote this letter.

Sixth, *the Jews had the promises.* These are still to be found in the pages of the Old Testament—promises of a time when the Jews would lead the nations of the world. From the Jews would come a universal reign, a world King, and Jerusalem would be the center of the earth. Government would flow from Jerusalem throughout the whole earth. These promises are still there, and God means to fulfill them.

Seventh, *the Jews had the patriarchs,* those tremendous men whose names are household words all over the world—Abraham, Moses, David, and others. Americans think we are blessed in having leaders like Washington, Jefferson, and Lincoln, but even they are not as widely known as these great names from Israel.

Finally, the supreme blessing was that *Jesus himself, the Messiah, came from Israel.* From the Jews is traced Christ's human ancestry. Paul does not say Christ belonged exclusively to Israel, but that he came *from* them. He belongs to the world because, as the apostle adds, "He is God over all, to be praised forever!" This is one of the clearest and most definite statements from the apostle's pen of the deity of Jesus. Some manuscripts suggest this is to be translated as a closing doxology: "God be blessed and praised forever." But the most ancient texts agree that the apostle wrote, "Christ is God over all, blessed and praised forever!"

Approaching Crisis

And yet with all these fantastic advantages, with their remarkable achievements and possibilities, the Jews of Paul's day were violently anti-Christian. They could not stand the idea of Jesus as their Messiah. Paul could see evidence, even at this early date, of the approaching crisis between the Jews and Romans that would result in Jerusalem's destruction and judgment upon the nation. They would be scattered throughout the world for centuries.

This letter was written about 53 A.D. Already events were moving to bring about a final confrontation in 70 A.D., when Roman armies would surround Jerusalem and break through its walls, destroy the temple, and take the Jews captive or drive them out into all the nations of the world—fulfilling the word of the Jesus they had rejected.

Now Paul raises a question that lies at the heart of this chapter: Since Israel has proved faithless, does this mean God also was faithless? Has God failed? Is he unable to save those he wants to save? This question is still relevant today, for many people wonder if God really can save someone he calls. Paul answers with a great statement trumpeting God's faithfulness—but in terms we struggle with.

I want to warn you, you'll have a difficult time with the ninth chapter of Romans. Way back in the prophet Isaiah's day, God said to Isaiah, "For my thoughts are not your thoughts, neither are your ways my ways. . . . For as the heavens are higher than the earth, so are my ways higher than your ways, and my thoughts than your thoughts" (Isaiah 55:8-9 RSV). Whatever else those words might mean, they certainly imply God sometimes acts in ways we don't understand, ways that seem absolutely contrary to how we think he should act.

Surely this is a major problem we face in seeking to understand God. At times I have been bewildered and baffled by God's behavior. I could see clearly how to work out certain problems—but God seemed unable to catch on. Even when I told him the simple steps (as I saw them) that would lead to a solution, he persisted instead in working it out by going into deeply involved relationships and circumstances with no apparent bearing on the problem. I am confronted, finally, with the truth of Isaiah's words. God is beyond me. This is the attitude we must have as we go through this chapter.

No Natural Advantages

Paul begins by showing us some of the principles by which God carries out his great work. The first is this: When God grants great opportunities and special privileges to people, this is no certain indication he guarantees to save them. Notice how Paul establishes his argument. First, he says, salvation is never based on natural advantages:

> *It is not as though God's word had failed. For not all who are descended from Israel are Israel. Nor because they are his descendants are they all Abraham's children (9:6-7).*

Two patriarchs are mentioned here, Abraham and Jacob (for Israel, of course, is another name for Jacob). After Jacob wrestled with the angel God renamed him Israel, for Israel means "A prevailer with God." God made Jacob, the usurper, into a conqueror. But his descendants are not necessarily involved in Jacob's promises. Even those who are physical descendants of Abraham, the greatest of the patriarchs, are not all included in God's salvation and reckoned as Abraham's true children.

Therefore, we can conclude that salvation is never based on natural advantages. It is not inherited. Your family may be Christian but that does not make you a Christian. You may have great opportunities for obtaining Bible knowledge, and perhaps you have taken advantage of them—but that does not make you a Christian. These special privileges are not the basis for God's redemption. This is the first thing we must understand. Ancestry does not guarantee redemption.

Rather, God's salvation is always based on a divine promise:

> On the contrary, "It is through Isaac that your
> offspring will be reckoned." In other words, it is
> not the natural children who are God's children,
> but it is the children of promise who are regarded
> as Abraham's offspring. For this was how the
> promise was stated: "At the appointed time I
> {God} will return, and Sarah will have a son"
> (9:7-9).

This takes us back to the eighteenth chapter of
Genesis, where God in effect said to Abraham and
Sarah, "I will come back, and Sarah, whose womb has
been barren all her life—who has never had a child,
who is now ninety years old, and who, from a natural
point of view, couldn't possibly have a child—is
going to have a baby." It was a biological miracle,
and this was God's promise. It involved his own
supernatural activity. His promise is based on what
he does, not on what men do.

Ishmael was Abraham's oldest son, thirteen years
older than Isaac. By his rights as the firstborn son he
should have inherited the promise God made to
Abraham. But instead, Isaac inherited this promise.
Ishmael stands forever as a symbol of the futility of
expecting God to honor our ideas of how he is to act.
Do you remember how Ishmael was born? Sarah said
to Abraham one day, "Do you expect God to do
everything? He has promised you a son, but you are
getting old. Time's wasting. Surely, God doesn't expect you to leave it all up to him!" So she suggested
he take her Egyptian servant as a concubine. He did,
and she conceived and bore a son. Abraham brought
Ishmael before God and said, "God, here is my son,
Ishmael. Will you fulfill your promises to him?" God
said, "No, I won't. He is not the one. I have promised
a son to Sarah and that son shall inherit the blessing
of Abraham."

Find the Promise

This is an important principle in Scripture. I meet many people who think they know what God ought to do. They misread the promises about prayer, for instance, and think if they pray for what they want, God has to grant it. But this account teaches that God is committed to do only what he has promised to do. If you want God to act on your behalf, find a promise he has given, and claim it in strict compliance to the conditions he has declared.

Many "faith healers" teach that God promises to heal all physical ailments. They tell people to "claim" healing from God. If we would just claim what God has promised, they say, God will do it. I have been studying the Scriptures for forty years or more, and I can't find that promise. God has never, anywhere, promised to heal all physical illnesses. He does heal, and often he will heal in response to the requests of his children—but he has never promised he will. We are wrong when we try to claim from God something he never promised. This is why anything expected from God must rest upon a promise he has already given. Otherwise it is wholly his grace that supplies an answer to our requests. That is the second principle here.

Now we come to the third principle, which is even more difficult to handle:

> Not only that, but Rebecca's children had one and the same father, our father Isaac. Yet, before the twins were born or had done anything good or bad—in order that God's purpose in election might stand: not by works but by him who calls—she was told, "The older will serve the younger" (9:10-12).

Remember Rebecca? She was Isaac's wife. He found her through Abraham's servant, who had been sent to find God's choice for him. Before their twin sons were born God told Rebecca the elder would serve the younger. This was a remarkable statement, and Paul confirms it with a quotation from Malachi 1:2-3.

> *Just as it is written, "Jacob I loved, but Esau I hated."*

Many have struggled over those words. But all the apostle is saying is that, first, ancestry does not make any difference (these boys had the same father); and second, what they will do in their lives—including the choices they make—ultimately will not make any difference. Before they were able to make choices either good or bad, God said to their mother, "The elder shall serve the younger." By this he implied not only a difference in the two nations descended from Jacob and Esau, but also a difference involving the *personal* destinies of these two men.

This is clear from history's record. Jacob forever stands for the faith God honors and wants men to have. Jacob was a scheming, weak character—not very lovable. Esau on the other hand was a rugged individualist—much more admirable than Jacob. But through the course of their lives, Jacob was brought to faith, and Esau was not.

A man once said to a noted Bible teacher, "I'm having trouble with this verse, 'Jacob I loved, but Esau I hated.' How could God ever say, 'Esau I hated'?"

The Bible teacher answered, "I have trouble with this verse too—but what bothers me is how God could ever say 'Jacob I loved'!" Read the life of Jacob and you will see why.

To Love Less

We must not read this word "hated" as though God actually detested Esau and treated him with contempt. This is what we often mean when we say we hate someone. Jesus used this same word when he said, "If anyone comes to me and does not hate his father and mother, his wife and children, his brothers and sisters—yes, even his own life—he cannot be my disciple" (Luke 14:26). Clearly he is not saying we have to treat our mothers and fathers and wives and children and our own lives with contempt and disrespect. He means we are to give him preeminence over all others. Hatred, in this sense, means to love less. We are to love others less than we love him.

God did not hate Esau in any absolute sense. In fact he blessed him. He made of him a great nation. He gave him promises which he fulfilled to the letter. What these verses imply is that God set his heart on Jacob, to bring him to redemption, and all Jacob's followers would reflect the possibilities of that. As Paul has argued already, they were not all saved by this heritage, but Jacob would forever stand for what God wants men to be, and Esau would forever stand as a symbol of what he does not like.

Do you know where the final confrontation of Jacob and Esau is recorded in the Scriptures? It was when Jesus stood before Herod the king. Herod was an Idumean, an Edomite, a descendant of Esau. Jesus was a descendant of Jacob. There, standing face to face, were Jacob and Esau! Herod has nothing but contempt for the King of the Jews, and Jesus will not open his mouth in Herod's presence. This is God's strange and mysterious way of dealing with humanity. Jacob and Esau represent contradictory lifestyles which can never merge.

Paul is teaching us here that God has a sovereign, elective principle which he carries out on his own terms. Here are those terms again:

First, salvation is never based on natural advantages. Never! What you are by background or inheritance does not enter into whether you are going to be redeemed.

Second, salvation is always based on a promise from God. This is why we are exhorted in the Scriptures to believe God's promises. In some mysterious way, redemption includes our necessity to be confronted with those promises and to give a willing and voluntary submission to them. Paul brings this up later in the chapter when he discusses the harmony (as far as we can understand it) between the free will of men and the sovereign choice of God.

Third, salvation never takes any notice of whether we are good or bad. Never! In behavior these children in Rebecca's womb were neither good nor bad, yet God chose Jacob and passed over Esau. Since in God's sight all children are born into a lost race, what difference could moral or immoral behavior make? These terms represent only human appraisals of outward behavior.

Now I want to ask you something: How do you react to what we have covered so far? Does something in you want to say, "God, this is unfair! It isn't right!"? Then relax, because you are normal. Something in all of us, called the flesh, reacts this way. Later in Romans 9 Paul handles this further, and we will face the issue squarely and find out all we can about God's apparent unfairness. But in the meantime, let us reverently accept that God is greater than we are. He knows more than we, he knows what he is doing, and everything he does is consistent with his character and his love. Whether we understand it or not, this is where it will all come out.

2
LET GOD
BE GOD

(Romans 9:14-33)

There was a time when almost everyone believed the earth was flat. It was a comfortable theory to live with—safe, easy to understand. Believing it did not make it true, but it made life easier to handle and more predictable. So as scientists began to say the earth was really round, contrary to the way it looked to everyone's eyes, and that it was spinning on its axis and floating in a great sea of space, people grew very upset.

Religious people especially were disturbed, for many believed with all their heart that the Bible taught the earth was flat. In fact, they would quote certain passages that seemed to indicate this. It was a long time before people began to realize the new evidence actually made God appear more wonderful and more powerful than he ever had before. People also began to discover certain verses and passages, overlooked before, that supported this new evidence. They could see how this new truth fit the context of biblical revelation.

Our problem when we come to a passage like Romans 9 is that many of us have grown up thinking God is flat—rather safe, easy to understand and predict, fitting comfortably into the pattern we have made for him. With God crammed into our little theological boxes, we find ourselves secure.

We have already learned how easy it is to misread God's actions. As we look at history or contemporary events or at what the Bible itself records about God's actions, we easily think God intends to do what he actually does not. God operates in line with certain principles—*his* principles—three of which we have already seen in Romans 9. God does not grant salvation on the basis of natural privileges he has bestowed, nor does he redeem apart from his promise to do so, nor does he save anyone on the basis of human works.

The Right to Choose

So what *is* the basis on which God chooses? Paul's answer, which we take up now in the second half of Romans 9, is that God's choice is based upon his sovereign right to choose. God has a right to choose whom he will. This is the final resolution of the problem.

> *What then shall we say? Is God unjust? Not at all! For he says to Moses,*
>
> *"I will have mercy on whom I have mercy,*
> *and I will have compassion on whom I*
> *have compassion."*

It does not, therefore, depend on man's desire or effort, but on God's mercy. For the Scripture says to Pharaoh: "I raised you up for this very purpose, that I might display my power in you and that my name might be proclaimed in all the earth." Therefore God has mercy on whom he wants to have mercy, and he hardens whom he wants to harden (9:14-18).

You may not like it, but the ultimate reason for God's choice of anyone is simply that God chose him. He chooses whom he wants.

This is the thing about God men dislike the most. God is sovereign. He is neither responsible nor answerable to anyone. He is totally, absolutely sovereign. We don't like this, because to us sovereignty is always connected with tyranny. To trust anyone with this kind of power is to put ourselves in the hands of someone who might destroy us, and we instinctively fight it. We fight it in our national life, in our family life, and in our individual relationships. We do not trust anyone with absolute power over us. The Constitution of the United States is based on this concept that no one can be trusted with absolute power. We have checks and balances built into our government. We divide it into three parts, and pit one against the others so they all watch each other. We believe even the best of men can't be trusted with absolute power.

It is no wonder, therefore, that when we come to the Scriptures and confront a God with absolute power, we become uneasy and troubled. But if God had to give an answer to anyone, that being or person to whom God had to account would really be God. The very idea of God is that he is sovereign. He does what he pleases, what he wants to do. We must get rid of the idea that his sovereignty will destroy us. It will not, at all. As we will see before this is over, his sovereignty is our only hope!

Paul says here that God declares his own sovereignty. God said to Moses, "I will have mercy on whom I have mercy, and I will have compassion on whom I have compassion." Moses was a great example of God's way of choosing someone to bless. Who was Moses that God should choose him? Moses was no one in himself. In fact, he was a murderer. On one occasion, in a fit of temper, he killed a man. Then instead of turning himself in for justice, he hid the body in the sand. He was a criminal and a fugitive from justice. For forty years he had been living in the desert, a nobody. No one had heard of him. But the Lord picked him up, made him his messenger, and gave him a name that became known throughout history. He set him in authority over the greatest kingdom the world at that time had ever seen, and used him in a remarkable way. Why? God chose to do so. He had the right to do it. Moses contributed nothing to his choice.

On the other hand, God also demonstrated his sovereignty with Pharaoh. He took a man no better than Moses (in fact, Scripture tells us God often places the basest of men in power; see Daniel 4:17) and put him on a throne and gave him authority over all of Egypt. When Moses confronted him, Pharaoh continued to resist God's will. God could have kept Pharaoh from resisting, but he didn't. He allowed him to do what all men do by nature—resist God. So Pharaoh held out against God in order, as this verse says, that God might demonstrate his power and attract the attention of men everywhere to his greatness.

That bothers us. We think anyone who boasts about his greatness, who tries constantly to get

people to notice how great he is, is a conceited braggart. We don't like such people, largely because we
are jealous of them. We want people to admire our
greatness!

In our consistent tendency to think of God as nothing but an enlarged man, we attribute to him our
own motives. When man seeks his own glory, he is
destructive. To elevate himself he must necessarily
put others down. But God—for the welfare and benefit of God's creatures—*must* demonstrate his greatness. The more they understand his goodness and
greatness and glory, the richer their lives will be, and
the more they will enjoy life. Jesus said, "This is eternal life, that they might know thee, the only true
God, and Jesus Christ, whom thou hast sent" (John
17:3 KJV). So when God invites men to consider his
glory and think about his greatness, it is not because
God's ego needs to be massaged, but because his creatures require this for their best welfare. God therefore
finds ways to do it, even using men to resist his will
so his greatness and power are displayed.

All the Bitter Charges

Paul's conclusion, therefore, is that God has mercy
on whom he wants to have mercy, and he hardens
whom he wants to harden. Immediately someone ob-
jects. We all feel this objection, I am sure. We object
in the same words as verse 19:

> One of you will say to me: "Then why does God
> still blame us? For who resists his will?"

In this brief statement are hidden all the accusations and bitter charges men bring against God: God
is responsible for all human evil! God ultimately is to
blame, not us! What does man do with the truth of
God's sovereignty, this essential truth about God's
nature? He uses it to blame God for all evil.

Verses 22-29 give us Paul's answer to this, and we will look at it in due time. But right now I want to examine this charge men bring against God. What it really says is, "All right, Paul. You say God uses men for whatever he wants to use them. Men cannot resist him. Pharaoh could not resist God's use of him. God used him to oppose what he sent Moses to do in Egypt. Pharaoh was merely an instrument in God's hands. So God uses men to do evil, then he turns around and blames them for the evil and punishes them for doing what he made them do! That's not just! That's not fair! God himself must agree it isn't fair to make someone do something and then punish him for doing it. That is offensive to the very sense of justice God himself gave us!"

Sounds logical, doesn't it? How do you answer logic like this?

Paul has four things to say in reply, and the first is found in verse 20. Basically he says, "All right, who-ever you are: You are charging God with injustice. You say he is not fair. Let's examine your credentials. By this charge you have already condemned God. Do you, a man, have the right to condemn your Creator?"

Who are you, O man, to talk back to God?
"Shall what is formed say to him who formed it,
'Why did you make me like this?'"

Take a look, Paul says: Compare and consider the difference between man and God. Here is man, finite (his knowledge and understanding is limited) and frail. He has limited strength. He lasts only a little while—a breath of air and he is gone. The record shows us man is not only finite and frail, but also foolish, despite all his logic. He makes atrocious blunders, even when he thinks he is doing right.

With all his claims to logic and reason, he ends up
making the most idiotic mistakes. Does this kind of
man dare stand up against the God who is mighty
and wise, absolute in power and majesty, infinite in
knowledge, knowing all things from beginning to
end—not only all things that are, but also all things
that could be? This puny pipsqueak of a man dares to
stand up and challenge the justice of a God like that?

Paul is saying even our logic is often wrong, because of mysteries we do not reckon on, objectives we
cannot discern, resistance we know nothing about.
So who are you, man, to stand and question the right-
ness of God?

It is a good argument, isn't it? Are we equipped to
challenge God in this way?

Look Who's Asking!

Perhaps the most helpful book in the Bible on this
score is Job. Job was not a cavalier; he was not a skep-
tic, an atheist arguing against God. He was a devout
man who loved God deeply. Yet he was a deeply bewildered man who could not understand what God
was doing with him. You know the story. Job was
afflicted with a series of terrible boils and physical af-
flictions, and his family and all his wealth disap-
peared in a triphammer series of terrible catas-
trophes.

To top it all, he was afflicted by three torturers
who called themselves his friends. Job's suffering,
they told him, meant he somehow was a deep-dyed
sinner, and all his pain was a result of refusing to let
people know the terrible evil he must have done.
They hounded poor Job, examining every crack and
cranny of their argument, plumbing to its depths.
Finally, in despair, Job cried out. He never once
blamed God—this is the glory of the book—but just

said, "Lord, I don't understand it! Oh, if I could just come and stand before you and plead my case, I could show you how unfair it seems to me!"

So in chapters 38 through 41, God appears to Job and says, "All right, Job, you wanted a chance to argue. You wanted to ask me questions. *Here I am.* But before you begin, I have questions for you, to see if you are qualified to investigate me. Here are my questions: Where were you when I laid the foundation of the earth? Where were you when the morning stars sang together, and I flung the heavens into space? Were you there? Can you enter into the secrets of the sea? Do you understand how rain works, and how lightning appears? Do you understand these things, Job? They are simple to me—what about to you?"

Job has to hang his head.

God goes on: "Look at the stars, Job. Can you order their courses? Can you make the Pleiades shine forth in the springtime? Can you make Orion stride across the winter sky, always on time? Can you handle the universe, Job?"

And Job says, "No, I'm sorry; I don't qualify."

God says, "All right, let me ask you more questions." And in a tremendous passage that is the real key to the book of Job, God uses the figures of Behemoth and Leviathan, two strange and formidable creatures, as he examines Job's qualifications to handle satanic power. "Can you handle Satan? Do you know how to control this fantastic dragon who can wreck a third of the universe with his tail? Are you able to take him on?"

Finally Job is on his face in the dust before God and says, "Lord God, I didn't know what I was getting into! I just meant to say a few things to you, but I am not in your league at all! I repent in sackcloth and ashes; I put my hand on my mouth. I have nothing to say to a God like you."

This is Paul's argument here in Romans 9: "Who are you, O man, to reply against God? You don't understand even a tiny fraction of the things to be known, so how can you argue with such a God?"

Delegated Sovereignty

Paul's second argument follows. Even among men, he says, we can see a rightful form of sovereignty in action.

> *Does not the potter have the right to make out of the same lump of clay some pottery for noble purposes and some for common use? (9:21).*

Nobody questions this, do they? Doesn't a potter have the right to divide a lump of clay in two, and make out of one half a beautiful vase for the living room and out of the other a slop jar? Why, yes, he has this right. No one tells the potter what he should do with his clay. Men exercise sovereignty like this and nobody questions it at all.

At this point many people say, "But we're not clay! It's all right to do that with unfeeling clay, but human beings are not clay. We're people. We have feelings, sensitivities, and wills. Your analogy doesn't hold!" Well, you can extend the analogy to living things. What about the ways we treat plants and animals? Doesn't a gardener have the right to move plants around wherever he pleases? Just last week I tore out some good healthy plants and threw them away. Did I have the right to do this? Should my neighbors swear out a warrant for my arrest because I didn't first ask permission of the plants? Does a farmer have the right to select certain cattle he thinks are nice and fat and send them to slaughter, while he keeps others a while longer? Would we ever challenge him? No. Men have this kind of authority—a kind of delegated sovereignty. Therefore, can we deny it to the One who, in all the created universe, has this right above all else? This is Paul's argument. And it is hard to refute, isn't it?

"But," someone says, "it still doesn't solve this problem of justice. It seems unfair." Paul's third argument says, "Then let us consider two possible motives in God's actions":

> *What if God, choosing to show his wrath and make his power known, bore with great patience the objects of his wrath—prepared for destruction? What if he did this to make the riches of his glory known to the objects of his mercy, whom he prepared in advance for glory—even us, whom he also called, not only from the Jews but also from the Gentiles? As he says in Hosea:*

> > *"I will call them 'my people' who are not*
> > > *my people;*
> > *and I will call her 'my loved one' who*
> > > *is not my loved one,"*

> *and,*

> > *"It will happen that in the very place*
> > > *where it was said to them {the Gen*
> > > *tiles},*
> > *'You are not my people,'*
> > *they will be called 'sons of the living God.'"*

> *Isaiah cries out concerning Israel:*

> > *"Though the number of the Israelites be*
> > > *like the sand by the sea,*
> > > *only the remnant will be saved.*

> *For the Lord will carry out his sentence*
> *on earth with speed and finality"*
> *(9:22-28).*

Paul says God may have purposes and objectives
we do not see. But doesn't he have the right to those
purposes? What if one of those objectives is not only
to display his power and his wrath by allowing man
to oppose him until he ultimately judges them, but
also to display his amazing patience and longsuffering? Did you ever think about that? Did you you ever
think how God for centuries and centuries has put up
with the snarling, nasty, blasphemous, accusing re-
marks of men, and done nothing to them? He has lis-
tened to all the cheap, shoddy, vulgar things men say
about him, and has allowed them to treat him with
hostility and anger, never doing a thing, but pa-
tiently enduring it.

Paul says, "What if God does all this? What if it
takes this kind of display of both the wrath of God
and the patience of God to bring those of us whom he
chooses to himself?" Something has to appear to us to
make us understand God. We are not forced to come
to him; we are drawn to him. Therefore we have to
respond, and something must make us respond. Is it
not the wrath of God (which reveals his power) and
the patience of God (which reveals his love) that draw
us to him?

All this, then, is necessary to bring some to glory.
In other words, for some to be saved, some must be
lost. I admit this is an inscrutable mystery, one I
don't understand. But I don't have to. That's the
whole thing. I cannot understand it right now.
Someday God will reveal certain other factors to help
us understand it, but he doesn't now—not because
he does not want to, but because I can't handle it and

neither can you. We have to accept it nevertheless. Paul suggests here that without the display of wrath on God's part, no Gentiles would have ever been saved—only the elect of Israel, and only a remnant of them. But as it is, the Gentiles, those of us who never had the advantages Israel had, are included, as Hosea and Isaiah both predicted.

The final and clinching argument, the fourth one, is found in verse 29:

It is just as Isaiah said previously:

"Unless the Lord Almighty
had left us descendants,
we would have become like Sodom,
and we would have been like Gomorrah."

I doubt any place on earth is more desolate than the sites of Sodom and Gomorrah—just dreary, dry desert beside a briny sea in which nothing will live and around which nothing will grow. Paul argues that if God had not chosen to draw us to himself by an elective decree—something that makes men wake up and stop resisting him and start listening to him—none of us would ever be saved.

Born Lost

Clearly, we start thinking on this problem from the wrong premise. We start by thinking that everyone is in neutral, and unless he has an opportunity to be saved, he remains in neutral until it is too late for him to have a chance. But that isn't it at all! The truth is, we were all born lost. We are already lost; we were lost in Adam. Adam lost the race, not we; but we are victims of his sin. None of us has a chance to do anything but resist God. Paul said in chapter 3, "There is none who does good, no, not one! There is none who seeks after God, not one!" God does not

shut us away without a chance. His grace reaches out
to us. Without it, no one at all would ever be saved.
The whole race would be lost. God's justice would
allow the race to be lost, but God's mercy reaches out
to save many among us. That properly is his
sovereign choice, and that is where we must leave it.

The passage closes with a remarkable paragraph.
At this point people ask, "How can we tell whether
someone is chosen or not? If you can't tell by the advantages they have, how can you tell?" Here is the
answer:

> *What then shall we say? That the Gentiles, who
> did not pursue righteousness, have obtained it, a
> righteousness that is by faith; but Israel, who
> pursued a law of righteousness, has not attained
> it. Why not? Because they pursued it not by faith
> but as if it were by works. They stumbled over the
> "stumbling stone." As it is written:*
>
> *"See, I lay in Zion a stone that causes men
>   to stumble
> and a rock that makes them fall,
> and the one who trusts in him will never
>   be put to shame" (9:30-33).*

God says you can tell whether you are being drawn
by the Spirit unto salvation or whether you are being
permitted by God to remain where you already were,
lost and condemned: You can tell it by what you do
with Jesus.

God has planted a stone in the middle of society's
path. When we walk down that path and come to this
big flat rock in the middle of it, we can either
stumble over it or stand on it—one or the other. God
says Jesus is that rock.

The Jews, who determined to work out their salvation on the basis of their own behavior, their own

good works before God, stumbled over the stone. This is why the Jews rejected Jesus, and why many of them reject him to this day. They don't want to admit they are unable to save themselves, and need a Savior. But those who see they need a Savior have already been drawn by the Spirit of God, awakened by his grace, and made to understand what is going on in their lives. Their very desire to be saved, their awareness of their need for a Savior, causes them to accept Jesus. They stand upon that stone. Anyone who comes on this basis will never be put to shame.

This, God says, is the testing point. The crisis of humanity is Jesus. You can be very religious, you can spend hours and days or an entire lifetime following religious pursuits and apparently honoring God. But the test will always come: What do you do with Jesus? God put him in society to reveal those whom he has called and those whom he has not. Jesus taught this very plainly: "No one can come to me unless the Father who sent me draws him . . . . All that the Father gives me will come to me, and whoever comes to me I will never drive away" (John 6:44,37).

So what is left for us? To respond to Jesus, that is all. And to thank God that in doing so, we are not only doing what our hearts and consciences urge us to do, but we are responding in obedience to the drawing of the electing Spirit of God, who in mercy has chosen to bring us out of a lost humanity.

3
HOW TO
BE SAVED

(Romans 10:1-13)

---

*Brothers, my heart's desire and prayer to God for
the Israelites is that they may be saved (10:1).*

I doubt any word in the Christian vocabulary
makes people more uncomfortable than the word
saved. People cringe when they hear it. Perhaps it
conjures up visions of hot-eyed, zealous button-
holers—usually with bad breath—who walk up and
grab you and say, "Brother, are you saved?" Or
perhaps it raises visions of a tiny band of Christians at
a street meeting in front of some saloon singing,
"Give the winds a mighty voice, Jesus saves! Jesus
saves!"

I will never forget the startled look on the face of a man who came up to me in a movie theater. The seat beside me was vacant, and he said, "Is this seat saved?" I said, "No, but I am." He promptly found a seat across the aisle. Somehow this word threatens our religious complacency and angers the self-confident and the self-righteous alike.

And yet, when you turn to the Scriptures this word is absolutely unavoidable. Christians *have* to talk about men and women being saved because the fact is that men and women are *lost*. There is no escaping it: The Bible teaches that the human race is a lost race. This is why John 3:16 is good news: "God so loved the world that he gave his one and only Son, that whoever believes in him shall not perish"—*not perish*—"but have eternal life." We can never deal realistically with life until we face up to this fundamental fact. People are not in the process of waiting until they die to be lost—they are already lost. The grace of God reaches down and calls us out of that lostness and gives us an opportunity to come to Christ and be saved. Therefore "saved" is a perfectly legitimate word.

Paul is explaining why some who have little knowledge are saved while many who have much knowledge are not. Part of his answer was given in the ninth chapter, in which he explained that behind this strange mystery is the elective, sovereign choice of God. God chooses to call men to him—but not all men. Now he turns to the other side. Now we are confronted with human responsibility. It is true God draws men to him; it is also true no one will come unless he voluntarily responds to the appeal of God.

As we have seen, human knowledge is too limited to resolve this apparent conflict. But both sides are true. God calls men by an elective decree that is irresistible, and yet they must respond by a choice of their will, which they are free to make or not, as it pleases them. Let's see how Paul introduces this other side of the picture and brings before us Israel's responsibility:

> *Brothers, my heart's desire and prayer to God for the Israelites is that they may be saved. For I can testify about them that they are zealous for God, but their zeal is not based on knowledge. Since they did not know the righteousness that comes from God and sought to establish their own, they did not submit to God's righteousness (10:1-3).*

Called through Our Prayers

Probably the most outstanding thing about this paragraph is this: Despite Paul's profound conviction that God saves whomever he will by an irresistible choice, nevertheless this does not stop Paul from praying and yearning over his kinsmen according to the flesh, the nation of Israel. Clearly, prayer is not inconsistent with God's call. It is never right for us to say, "If God calls, there is nothing for us to do," because the way God calls is through the preaching of the Word and the praying of Christians, the yearning of their hearts over those who are not yet saved. Therefore, this is all part of God's program, and we need to see the importance such prayer has in reaching people. Paul prayed for men. In 1 Timothy 2:1-4,8 he writes,

> *I urge, then, first of all, that requests, prayers, intercession and thanksgiving be made for everyone—for kings and all those in authority, that we may live peaceful and quiet lives in all*

*godliness and holiness. This is good, and pleases
God our Savior, who wants all men to be saved
and to come to a knowledge of the truth I
want men everywhere to lift up holy hands in
prayer, without anger or disputing.*

Prayer is a great factor in this call, as C. S. Lewis
has pointed out:

*When we are praying about the result, say, of a
battle or a medical consultation, the thought will
often cross our minds that, if we only knew it, the
event is already decided one way or the other. I
believe this to be no reason for ceasing our prayers.
The event certainly has been decided. In a sense,
it was decided before all the worlds. But one of
the things taken into account in deciding it, and
therefore one of the things that really causes it to
happen, may be this very prayer that we are now
offering. . . . Thus, shocking as it may sound,
I conclude that we can at noon become part causes
of an event occurring at ten o'clock.*

Even our prayers *after* an event affect the event.
This is strange to us, but I think it is true. We are up
against a great mystery in the matter of prayer. Lewis
adds:

*There is no question whether an event has hap-
pened because of your prayer. When the event you
prayed for occurs, your prayer has always contributed to it. When the opposite event occurs,
your prayer has never been ignored; it has been
considered and refused for your ultimate good and
the good of the whole universe.*

These are deep matters, but at least it is clear Paul
does not hesitate to pray, though he knows God
chooses whom he will.

The second emphasis Paul makes in this paragraph is Israel's zeal. "I can testify about them that they are zealous for God." And indeed they are. Perhaps the most noteworthy difference between an orthodox Jew and the average Gentile is right there. Jews take God seriously. Any of you who have seen *Fiddler on the Roof* or read the writings of Chaim Potok know how true this is. The Jewish way of life is built around God. God is the most important element in their thinking. They sacrifice anything and everything to the centrality of God in their national and community life.

This is in stark contrast to the average Gentile. Gentiles have religious feelings—all men do. Gentiles think of God, but God is on the periphery of Gentile life. I think we Gentiles often demonstrate this. We are more casual about God. He is not the center of life, as he is in Jewish thought and action.

Yet what amazes Paul, and amazes us today, is that the casual Gentile, who is not necessarily looking for God, nevertheless often finds him. He discovers God suddenly intruding into his life when he didn't expect him. He finds peace and rest and joy even when he isn't looking for them. But the Jew, with all his zeal, with his consummate desire to discover and to know God, fails to find peace and forgiveness and is not reborn into joy and love.

To Establish Their Own

Paul tells us why this is so: The Jews sought to establish their own righteousness, and therefore missed the gift of God, which is the righteousness of Christ, obtained without works. Anyone, Jew or Gentile, who seeks to establish his own righteousness, will be in the same boat. The Jews were constantly trying their best to obey the law of Moses. They were failing to do so, of course, but they were not willing to admit

they failed. They kept hoping and seeking and believing God would accept them, though they did not
truly obey the law.

Many people are like this today, both Jew and
Gentile. In fact, to show you how Jews still think this
way, I will quote from a letter sent by a rabbi to a boy
I know, a boy with a Jewish background. The rabbi
wrote because he was troubled about the boy's faith
in Christ.

> *The basic question about religion is how to elevate*
> *man, and bring him into closer relationship with*
> *God. We believe that God revealed to us in the*
> *Torah {the law of Moses} how he wants us to*
> *live, so that we can be in harmony with his divine*
> *purpose. Our role and religious purpose is to obey*
> *God's laws—to love him and to obey him. We*
> *exercise our free will by proper intention and,*
> *through having done the good deeds, are elevated*
> *so that it becomes progressively easier and more*
> *natural to continue to do good and to resist evil.*

This is the current Jewish view of how to be right
before God—simply keep trying until it becomes
easier and easier, and finally you stand righteous before God. Paul says this is the problem; anyone who
seeks to come before God on this basis is doomed to
failure. Such persons do not and cannot obey the law.
Paul goes on to show us why they can't, and reveals
to us that the issue is always Jesus.

> *Christ is the end of the law so that there may be*
> *righteousness for everyone who believes (10:4).*

Christ is the end of the law—any kind of law—so
that there may be righteousness for everyone who believes. Of course this does not mean Christ does away
with law. He does away with law as far as its effect in

bringing you to God is concerned. He makes a total end of it. And as we have seen in this letter, the reason is clear. What was the purpose of law? To make us aware something is wrong with us! If you don't have a standard to try to live up to, you have no idea anything is wrong with you. You think everything you do is natural, and therefore right. We hear this argument all the time: Anything natural is right. This is because more and more today the law is being set aside.

The law was given to make us realize there are things that feel natural that are wrong. These things are destroying us. All the injury and death and darkness in our lives come because of our actions and attitudes. *We* produce the problem. We think it comes from everyone else, but the law helps us see we are wrong. But once it has shown us, then what good is it? It can do no more.

At this point, unless we come to Christ, we have no way out. The law cannot cure our evil; it can only show it to us. The law becomes our schoolmaster to bring us to Christ, as Paul puts it in Galatians 3:24. This is the end of the law; this is its purpose. It has been fulfilled when it does this work and brings you to Jesus Christ. He can change you. He can give you new life. He can wipe out the old pattern of failures and all the hurt and agony and anguish you have been going through, and give you a wholly new heart. Therefore Christ is the end of law, that there may be righteousness to everyone who believes in him.

In his logical way, Paul is careful to show us how this works. He quotes Moses to prove what the law is for:

> *Moses describes in this way the righteousness that is by the law: "The man who does these things {fulfills the law} will live by them" (10:5).*

Moses said in Exodus and Leviticus: "Here is the law, the Ten Commandments. Anybody who does these things will live. God will bless him, fulfill his humanity, make him enjoy all that God had for man in the beginning. It will all come if a man will simply obey these ten rules." You know, when you read the Ten Commandments, they always seem so reasonable, they seem so easy to obey. This is the way people have always reacted to them. You say to yourself, "Why, this is not difficult. I can easily do these. All I have to do is just decide to do it, that's all!" But when you actually start to do it, you soon discover a rebelliousness inside that sooner or later stops you from doing what you want to do.

We have seen this all through Romans. So it ends up that the law was given to make people try to live this way. Paul said he who did these things would live.

The Gospel According to Moses

Now Paul goes on to quote Moses again. He doesn't say Moses said the next part, but he did, in the book of Deuteronomy. Paul sets the faith way to God right next to the law way:

> But the righteousness that is by faith says: "Do not say in your heart, 'Who will ascend into heaven?'" (that is, to bring Christ down), "or 'Who will descend into the deep?'" (that is, to bring Christ up from the dead). But what does it say? "The word is near you; it is in your mouth and in your heart," that is, the word of faith we are proclaiming (10:6-8).

It may startle you to realize Paul is saying Moses taught salvation by grace through faith, just as Paul did. Moses knew the law would not work. Even as he was bringing the tablets down from the mountaintop the people had broken all ten of the commandments before the law was given to them. And after they received them they promptly broke them again.

Moses knew the people could not keep them, but Moses also taught that God had provided another way by which people could be delivered when they failed. He saw that God would lay the foundation for salvation in the incarnation, crucifixion, and resurrection of Jesus. This is why Paul quotes these words from Deuteronomy. Moses foresaw the coming of Christ from heaven, and he saw the resurrection, the raising of Jesus from the dead. Paul clearly indicates God all along had this basis in mind as the way people were to come to Christ.

When the angels sang their song to some shepherds in the darkness of the night on the plains of Bethlehem, and the glory of the Lord broke out upon them in the fields, the angel of the Lord said to them, "Behold, I bring you good tidings of great joy, which shall be to all people; for unto you is born this day in the city of David a Savior, who is Christ the Lord" (Luke 2:10,11 KJV). This was the historic fulfillment of the way God had been saving people for centuries before this. Now it is being worked out in history—but God had long before been saving people who saw beyond the law to the work of Christ.

When the angels, in the brightness of the Easter sunrise, said to the woman at the tomb of Jesus, "Go and tell his disciples that he is risen, as he said," this was the culmination of God's program to work out human redemption quite apart from any effort on man's part. Jesus had done it all. So Paul points out here that Moses understood the way to lay hold of and to personally appropriate the value of these incredible events: to believe the divine announcement with the whole man, with the whole being. Thus he adds,

> *But what does it say? "The word is near you; it is in your mouth and in your heart," that is, the word of faith we are proclaiming (10:8).*

The mouth symbolizes the outward man, the intellectual understanding of what has happened expressed in words; the heart is the inner man, the will, the spirit deep within us which understands the basis on which God saves. Lest anyone miss his point, Paul goes on with these clear words:

> *If you confess with your mouth, "Jesus is Lord," and believe in your heart that God raised him from the dead, you will be saved. For it is with your heart that you believe and are justified, and it is with your mouth that you confess and are saved (10:9-10).*

This is the clearest statement in God's Word on how to be saved. Paul makes it simple. He says it begins with the confession of the mouth that "Jesus is Lord."

Right to Lordship

Paul does not mean you have to stand up in public somewhere and announce your belief that Jesus is Lord before you are saved, although what he says does not exclude that. He views the mouth as the symbol of a conscious acknowledgment to ourselves of what we believe. It means we have come to the place where we recognize Jesus has the right to lordship in our lives. Up to this point we have been lord of our lives. We have run our own affairs, feeling we have the right to make our own decisions according to what we want. But in time, as God's Spirit works in us and we see the reality of life as God has made it, we realize Jesus is Lord. He is Lord of our past, forgiving us our sins; he is Lord of our present, dwelling within us and guiding, directing, and controlling every area of our life; he is Lord of our future, leading us into glory at last. Christ is Lord of life, Lord of death, Lord over all.

As Jesus himself said after his resurrection, "All power is given unto me, in heaven and on earth"—*all* power. Jesus is in control of history; he is running all human events. He stands at the end of every path on which men go, and he is the ultimate One we all must reckon with. This is why Peter says in Acts 4:12, "Salvation is found in no one else; for there is no other name under heaven given to men by which we must be saved." You cannot read the book of Acts without recognizing that the basic creed of the early Christians was "Jesus is Lord."

These days one hears much about mantras, words one is supposed to repeat when meditating. But mantras have a dulling effect; they are more likely to fog your mind than they are to sharpen your wits. I suggest rather that we adopt a truly significant phrase to ponder: Jesus is Lord. Wherever you are, say it again and again, to remind yourself of this great truth. When Peter stood up to speak on the day of Pentecost, this was his theme—"Jesus is Lord." The thousands of Jews listening to him could not deny what he pointed out: Jesus had lived a unique life, was witnessed to by the prophets before him, died a remarkable death, was raised from the dead in an astonishing way, then poured out supernatural signs from heaven—evidences they could not deny. They had to recognize the fact above all facts, whether they liked it or not: Jesus is Lord. The great question of all time is therefore, "What are you going to do with Jesus?"

Paul tells us Jesus is Lord, and if you have believed in your heart that he is risen and available and you are ready to say to yourself, "Jesus is *my* Lord," then God acts. At this moment God does something. No man can do it, but God can. He begins to bring about all that is wrapped up in this word "saved." Your sins will be forgiven; God imparts to you a standing of righteous worth in his sight; he loves you; he gives you the Holy Spirit to live within you; he makes you a son in his family; he gives you an inheritance for eternity; you are joined to the body of Christ as members of the family of God; you are given Jesus himself to live within you, to be your power over evil, over the world, the flesh, and the devil; and you will live in an entirely different way than before. This is what happens when you confess with your mouth that Jesus is Lord and believe in your heart that God raised him from the dead.

He Becomes Savior

Nowhere in all the Scriptures are we ever asked to believe in Jesus as Savior; we are asked to believe in him as Lord. When you believe in him as Lord, he becomes your Savior. But you don't accept Christ as a Savior—you accept him as Lord, as the one in charge of all things, including you. When you can respond with the whole man, then God says the work of redemption is done. The miracle occurs.

"Well," someone says, "what if I'm not elect? What if all the time I've been wanting God and seeking God, and then it turns out I'm not chosen?" Anyone who talks this way (and people do talk this way) shows he has never understood what Paul is saying here. For if you believe in Christ you have given proof that you are elect. As Jesus himself put it, "No one can come to me unless the Father who sent me draws him." You can't believe in God until God has called you and drawn you. The very desire to believe is part of that drawing, therefore we needn't struggle over this apparent conflict.

What Scripture everywhere confronts us with is the necessity for everyone to settle the question, "Is Jesus Lord of my life?" Is he your Lord? Have you enthroned him and acknowledged him where God has placed him, as King over all the earth, the Lord of glory, the one who is in charge of all things? When you do, this is the moment redemption begins to occur. Notice how Paul confirms this, first quoting Isaiah:

As the Scripture says, "Everyone who trusts in him will never be put to shame."

It is not on the basis of works, but of belief: He who accepts what Christ does, who believes on him, will not be put to shame. Paul goes on:

> *For there is no difference between Jew and*
> *Gentile—the same Lord is Lord of all*
> *and richly blesses all who call on him,*
> *for, "Everyone who calls on the name of*
> *the Lord will be saved" {words from the*
> *prophet Joel} (10:12-13).*

These verses indicate this is not something new with Paul, but something taught by all the Scriptures, Old and New Testaments alike: Faith is the way we lay hold of what God has to give us. It is never gained by earning it or by trying to be good, or by our good outweighing our bad, but simply by acknowledging that Jesus Christ has done it all on our behalf, and by opening our hearts to his lordly control.

John 1:11-12 tells us, "He came to that which was his own, but his own did not receive him. Yet to all who received him, to those who believed in his name, he gave the right to become children of God." So if you have asked him to come into your heart and received him as Lord, and you mean to allow him to be the controlling center of your life, I can tell you on the authority of the Word of God: You have been saved!

4
HAVE THEY
NOT HEARD?

(Romans 10:14-21)

This section of Romans 10 answers one of the questions non-Christians ask most frequently, in various forms: "What happens to all the people who never hear about Jesus?" The question especially concerns them when they hear Christians claiming that Jesus is the only way to God.

In the first part of the chapter, the apostle declared that to be salvaged from the wreck of humanity, a man or woman must call upon the name of the Lord. But how do you call on the name of the Lord? Paul goes on in verse 14 to outline the steps that lie behind this essential to salvation.

How, then, can they call on the one they have not believed in? And how can they believe in the one of whom they have not heard? And how can they hear without someone preaching to them? And how can they preach unless they are sent? As it is written, "How beautiful are the feet of those who bring good news!" (10:14-15).

Five steps are outlined here in calling on the name of the Lord. Paul begins with the final step, the call itself. He traces it back so we can see what is involved in bringing people to the place where they cry out to God and are saved, born again, made alive in Jesus Christ.

To begin, Paul stresses that each person individually must call on God. "*Everyone* who calls on the name of the Lord will be saved." The conviction and call must be individual and personal. It is not enough to sit under the preaching of the gospel. Some think if they go to church regularly and hear the gospel they will be saved. No, a time must come when one calls personally on the name of the Lord.

Beyond Emotions

Before the call is belief. Paul says, "How, then, can they call on the one they have not believed in?" There must be belief. This means the mind must be engaged—the intellect is called into play. This is important because many people are stirred emotionally, but understand little about what God has done. They have nothing to believe in; they are simply stirred up to want something.

Years ago a great English-born evangelist named Gypsy Smith used to preach up and down this country. I remember Dr. H. A. Ironside saying Gypsy Smith once came to Moody Church in Chicago and in a series of meetings told about his boyhood conversion and his gypsy background. The people would sit entranced with the wonderful stories he told. At the end of the meeting he would give an altar call, and people would surge forward in great numbers. Dr. Ironside said he used to wonder why they were coming. Did they want to be gypsies, or what? They had really been given nothing in which to believe. I well recall Dr. Lewis Sperry Chafer, my great teacher at Dallas Seminary, saying to us in class, "Men, remember, you have never preached the gospel until you have given people something to believe, something God has done that their minds can grasp, something leading them to understand what God has offered to them: their salvation."

Before belief, Paul says, is the message—something heard. "How can they believe in the one of whom they have not heard?" Something must be preached. Some message must be given. Again, this is an important aspect of Christian faith. We hear of new isms, new cults springing up on every side, dominating the religious field. Often they make their appeal to some mystical feeling or philosophy, some idea men have of what might bring them to God. But the glory of Christianity is that its message is grounded in history. It is objective truth, not merely something you feel inside of you. It is not some emotion you follow, hoping life somehow will work out; it is the story of historic events.

One of these events is the coming of Jesus as a baby in the manger at Bethlehem, followed by the arrival of the wise men from the east, causing an uproar in Judea, beginning with Herod the king himself. It is all part of history. Then came the crucifixion and the resurrection and all that followed in the church.

These are all historic events—objectively true. The Christian faith is grounded in events that cannot be explained away. This is the message we declare.

Human Messengers

Before the message, of course, is the messenger. "How can they hear without someone preaching to them?" A messenger must speak forth the message. God has always used some object or person to convey truth, and this method will never be superseded. All the marvelous communication media we have today are ways of conveying the preaching of the Word of God. You can preach today on television, on radio, by cassette tapes, and by video tapes. You can have the message flung to satellites and back to the four corners of the earth. But in every event, someone must deliver the message. God has chosen preaching as his means of conveying this great truth to every generation.

This is why distribution of the written Scriptures alone will never be sufficient to win men. I do not demean this ministry, because translating and spreading the Scriptures over the earth are important. But they are only supplementary to preaching. Alone they will never reach and change nations as does the gospel proclaimed by a human messenger. God has sent men everywhere to preach this Word and to proclaim the truth.

But before the messenger is the sender. "How can they preach unless they are sent?" There need be no doubt as to the One who does the sending. Jesus himself said, "Pray the Lord of the harvest, that he may send forth laborers." It is God who sends men. The great initiative in the process of redeeming men and women, of healing them and restoring them, comes from the heart of God. He calls out men and women and sends them to the far reaches of the earth.

Paul has surely brought all this before us so we might understand what a wonderful and beautiful thing God has done. This is why Paul quotes Isaiah here: "How beautiful are the feet of those who bring good news!" What a welcome and beautiful thing it is to think of God sending out men and women all over the earth with this message. How marvelous it is when this message takes root in the human heart! We never forget the ones who bring it to us. "How beautiful are the feet . . . ." Feet are not usually the most beautiful part of the body, but even they become beautiful when the gospel message is conveyed and God delivers, frees, and makes us whole.

Calling on the name of the Lord is like turning on a light switch. You flip the switch on the wall and the lights go on. It seems to be such a simple thing. Yet behind it is a complicated process: the power stations, the transmission towers, the substations, the dam built to hold back the water, the poles on which the wires are strung. A tremendous complexity lies behind the simple act of turning on a light switch. Every time you do it, power surges forth—but it comes only because of a complicated process already in existence.

Every time an individual comes to the place where in quietness he calls out to the Lord, a tremendous process is behind it: the birth of Jesus at Bethlehem, the darkness, anguish, and mystery of the cross, the wonder and miracle of the resurrection, the sending forth of the Holy Spirit on the day of Pentecost—all this is the process behind a single individual's call upon the name of the Lord. God is behind it all and has arranged it. The apostle wants us to understand this marvelous activity of the sovereign God.

Puzzle of Unbelief

But what if all this is provided, but still men do not respond? This is the problem Paul faces here in regard to Israel:

> *But not all the Israelites accepted the good news. For Isaiah says, "Lord, who has believed our message?" Consequently, faith comes from hearing the message, and the message is heard through the word of Christ (10:16-17).*

People often react strangely when they hear this message. It is what we might call the puzzle of unbelief. It is strange how some seem suspicious, so self-dependent that even when good news comes they don't want to receive it. Those who tell the good news run into this reaction all the time.

A young friend living in Fresno, California, once told me the story of his conversion. He was a man of considerable wealth, and he tried to reach his friends for Christ after he himself became a Christian. With tremendous enthusiasm he told them what had happened to him and how the Lord had changed his life and saved his marriage. But he found for the most part that his words fell on deaf ears. His wealthy friends patted him on the back and went their way.

Finally he decided on a rather strange and remarkable demonstration—both for his sake and the sake of his friends. He sat down and wrote out a check for a million dollars (and he was good for it, too!). Then he took his check around to his friends and said, "I have always regarded you highly as a friend. I have always wanted to do something for you. Would you receive this check as a gift from me?" When they saw the amount of the check, they would hand it back and say, "I can't take that from you." He tried to give the check out to a dozen or more of his friends and no one would take it, although it was a valid offer. Finally he faced the fact that something deeply embedded in human nature does not want to receive good news, does not want to be helped too much, does not want to be the recipient of great riches without having had some part in it.

The prophet Isaiah discovered this when he came to the people of Israel at a time when they were surrounded by enemies. They had turned to worship idols. Degrading practices had come into the nation's life, and peace and joy had fled from the land. In those dark days, 725 years before Christ was born, Isaiah came and preached to this people good news about One who was coming. He declared that on the basis of this person's life and death, God would work out their salvation. But he had to confess, as Paul writes here, that they would not believe his message.

The great and luminous fifty-third chapter of Isaiah begins with these words;

> *Who has believed our message*
> *and to whom has the arm of the LORD been*
> *revealed?*
> *He grew up before him like a tender shoot,*
> *and like a root out of dry ground.*
> *He had no beauty or majesty to attract us to him,*
> *nothing in his appearance that we should*
> *desire him.*
> *He was despised and rejected by men,*
> *a man of sorrows, and familiar with*
> *suffering.*
> *Like one from whom men hide their faces*
> *he was despised, and we esteemed him not.*
> *Surely he took up our infirmities*
> *and carried our sorrows,*
> *yet we considered him stricken by God,*
> *smitten by him, and afflicted.*

But he was pierced for our transgressions,
   he was crushed for our iniquities;
the punishment that brought us peace was
     upon him,
   and by his wounds we are healed.
We all, like sheep, have gone astray,
   each of us has turned to his own way;
and the LORD *has laid on him*
   the iniquity of us all.

Yet when Isaiah's stricken Sufferer came to the nation of Israel, it said no to him and refused the tremendous revelation of Isaiah the prophet—at least, most of the Israelites did.

Now Paul isolates the problem for us in verse 17 of Romans 10: "Consequently faith comes from hearing the message, and the message is heard through the word of Christ." This is a more accurate translation than the King James Version, which says, "and hearing comes by the word of God." It is really the word of Christ. Paul says faith is aroused by hearing. If you hear a message, you either must believe it or disbelieve it. Your faith is aroused by the message. But if it is to be saving faith, it must be a word about Christ. All Scripture is about Christ. As Jesus himself said, "You search the Scriptures . . . and they bear testimony to me."

Once again, Paul sets Jesus at the center of the universe. He is the great issue of life. Even in ancient Israel, hearing the news about Jesus precipitated "the puzzle of unbelief." People refused it, and the word "refused" brings the whole project of God's attempt to reach men to a point of failure.

Two Views of Messiah

Earlier we saw a section from a letter written by a rabbi to a boy of Jewish background who is now a

Christian. In his letter the rabbi also explained the difference he saw between what Jews and Christians believe about the Messiah. Perhaps you would be interested in his words:

> *The Messiah question is central to Christianity. This is the hub around which their whole theology rotates. To make this your major concern is to play their game. We have a belief in a messiah, but this is not too rigidly defined, nor of central concern. According to our belief, the messiah is a man, descended from the house of David, since God had promised not to replace the line of David with another, who will defeat the enemies of the Jews, restore the people to the land of Israel, rebuild the temple in Jerusalem, and reign there and introduce an era of peace. The advent of the messiah has to do with God's plan for actualizing his plans in the world.*

This is the usual Jewish position regarding the Messiah. He was to be a man, not divine; he was to come into history only to deliver the Jews from their oppressors, in fulfillment of the promises to Israel of leadership among the nations. But they ignore passages such as Isaiah 53 and others that speak of the suffering of the Messiah. The rabbi goes on,

> *The situation is quite different for the Christian. He believes that nothing that men do can help. Man necessarily exists in a state of sin. Ethical living, obedience to God, goodness, all are of no avail. The only way that a man can get out of a state of damnation is to believe that Jesus is his Savior or Messiah. Thus the whole purpose of religion is for man to be in Jesus i.e., to accept this belief in Jesus as his Savior.*

This betrays a considerable degree of understanding of the Christian position and of the gospel. The thoroughness of his understanding shows in his further words:

> *The Law (to a Christian) is not only ineffective, but unnecessary, because once one has accepted Jesus, one of the by-products is that he is essentially good and needs no direction from the Law. From this point of view, one of the most basic and almost exclusive concerns of religion is the Messiah. Don't be shifted to that question without realizing the difference in import and meaning that places messiah, as used by a Jew, and Messiah, as used by a Christian, worlds apart.*

This is the position Jews still take today regarding Christ. Paul says it was the issue in his day as well. The word he preached was the word of Christ which had power to awaken faith in one who received it.

Nature's Witness

But someone may say, "The Jews never really heard the gospel. Perhaps the problem is that it never reached them." This brings up the question about those who never hear. Paul takes this up at verse 18:

> *But I ask, Did they not hear? Of course they did:*
>
> *"Their voice has gone out into all the*
> *   earth,*
> *their words to the ends of the world."*

Psalm 19, from which Paul quotes here, details nature's witness to God. It begins,

> *The heavens declare the glory of God;*
> *   the skies proclaim the work of his hands.*
> *Day after day they pour forth speech;*
> *   night after night they display knowledge.*

> *There is no speech or language*
>> *where their voice is not heard.*
> *Their voice goes out into all the earth,*
>> *their words to the ends of the world.*

The gospel already has been universally proclaimed through nature. This is not much light about God, but it is light. Paul mentioned this witness in the first chapter of Romans:

> *What may be known about God is plain to them, because God has made it plain to them. For since the creation of the world God's invisible qualities—his eternal power and divine nature—have been clearly seen, being understood from what has been made, so that men are without excuse (1:19-20).*

Here is the answer to the question, "What about those who have never heard about God?" There aren't any people who have never heard about God! Men and women everywhere know something about him. He is revealed in nature. A universal proclamation has gone out. And if it is observed, if it is noticed and followed, more light will be given. Thus Hebrews 11, the great faith chapter, gives us the simplest declaration of how men come to God:

> *Anyone who comes to him must believe that he exists and that he rewards those who earnestly seek him (Hebrews 11:6).*

First, there must be belief, or faith in God's existence. Then one must believe God rewards men who diligently seek him. All men everywhere are responsible to seek the God who is revealed in nature. They may have no more light than this, but if they are obedient to it, it's enough to bring them (through gradually increasing light) to the knowledge of

Christ. God will see to it that they have further light. Israel had this proclamation. No matter how low they sank in their understanding, no matter how dark the land became, they at least had a universal proclamation of truth that could have brought them back to God.

But the revelation of God has another stage. God in his grace often gives more light even when people refuse the light of nature. No one deserves more light, but God gives it nevertheless. I think people in the United States of America above all peoples ought to be grateful for the grace God has poured out on us when we did not deserve it. God has given us much light. But we must remember that more light does not necessarily mean more belief. To make the light brighter does not mean people will believe more than when it was dim. Unbelief can reject bright light as well as dim light, so more light does not necessarily mean more belief. Thus the United States, with this great and shining light pouring so brilliantly upon it, is still a nation filled with unbelievers as was Israel of old.

Beyond the revelation of God in nature, God sends messengers:

Again I ask, did Israel not understand? First, Moses says,

"I will make you envious of those
who are not a nation;
I will make you angry by a nation that
has no understanding."

Then Isaiah boldly says,

"I was found by those who did not seek me;
I revealed myself to those who did not ask
for me" (10:19-20).

God sent the prophets to Israel. He sent Moses and Samuel, Elijah and Elisha, Isaiah and Jeremiah, and all the other prophets of the Old Testament. Through many years and centuries he sent them to this people. He did it to arouse them to jealousy, for although Israel often rejected the prophets, the Gentiles would often believe, as in the cases of Rahab and Naaman. This would be true more fully in the day when Gentile nations would turn to God in large numbers while the Jews remained hardened.

This, of course, is exactly what has happened. Paul singles out what God uses to arouse belief, even when people tend to reject truth—*jealousy*. I was watching my grandson play with his cousins one day. He was playing with a certain toy until he became tired of it and threw it away. One of his cousins picked it up and started playing with it, and immediately my grandson ran over and grabbed the toy away. "No, that's mine!" he said. He wanted to play with it only because he was made jealous by someone else having it.

Certainly God fully understands this principle of fallen human nature. He sometimes uses it to make people wake up. This is why God may open the eyes of one member of a family to receive spiritual insight. He does it to make the others jealous so they will listen to him. God will pour out blessings upon one nation to make other nations jealous. "What is the secret of your blessing?" they will ask. Thus they are awakened to the witness about God.

If you understand these things you will read your newspaper differently than you ordinarily do. What is God doing in the great human conflicts of our day? We may see them simply as encounters between warring factions, but God uses these events to arouse people to jealousy.

Paul gives two instances of this. First he points out what Moses said: God would use a people far less intelligent than the Jews. One of the striking things about Jewish history is their brilliance. It would be impossible to list all the Jewish leaders in science, philosophy, literature, art, and music. They dominate these fields. More than twelve percent of the Nobel Prize winners have been Jewish. And yet these brilliant people are often brought into contact with even untaught savages from the jungles who have found God, become Christians, been delivered from evil, and been blessed with hope, peace, and even prosperity. God is doing this to arouse and awaken his people.

Then, Paul declares, Isaiah came along. Not only will God use those who are less intelligent, he says, but God will use people who are less motivated: "I was found by those who did not seek me; I revealed myself to those who did not ask for me." Another characteristic of the Jew has been his zeal for God, as Paul has already pointed out. And yet careless Gentiles, who do not often think about God, learn through Christ to revel in the grace, love, and blessing of the living God. This is all to arouse Jews to jealousy. God uses this principle with Gentiles too. This explains why people watch Christians. A blessing is visible that non-Christians can't understand. God is using it to awaken them to listen, that they might be saved, to turn and settle the issue of salvation at the feet of Jesus.

A Four-Thousand-Year Day

A final stage of divine pursuit is described in verse 21:

> But concerning Israel he says,
> "All day long I have held out my hands
> to a disobedient and obstinate people."

What a beautiful picture of God's character. Here is declared his remarkable patience—"all day long"! That day has stretched now for almost four thousand years. Four thousand years ago Abraham set out for Canaan. Four thousand years later, God is still holding out his hands to this stubborn people, longing to draw them to himself.

He is not only patient, but loving. He holds out his hands! This is the stance of God toward those who resist his will—with wide open arms, all day long, he waits to draw them back.

Remember that Jesus said to the Pharisees of his day, "You will not come unto me that you may have life." Looking over Jerusalem, he wept as he saw the stubbornness and pride of people who will not admit their need. This has been repeated again and again throughout the world. God longs to draw men to himself. He must somehow arouse faith in the individual. To do so he sends messengers with a glorious message, and yet his will and purpose meet resistance.

Romans 10 closes with this picture of God— standing with open arms, longing to draw men to himself, stating that the problem is a disobedient and obstinate people. The most amazing thing from this account is to realize that in order to perish, to go to hell, you must resist the pleas of a loving God. God never damns anyone to hell without a chance, and don't let anyone tell you the Bible teaches that he does. The Bible does not teach any such thing.

Rather, it teaches us that no one—not one person—will end up separated from God who has not personally resisted the claim and appeal of the loving God who sought to reach him. Hell is arrived at only after long years of rejecting truth and turning one's back to the light.

5
THERE'S HOPE AHEAD

(Romans 11:1-24)

The eleventh chapter of Romans deals with Israel—its hope, its promises, and its relationship to the church. Unfortunately the church and Israel are often like two relatives who can't get along. Through the centuries, disagreement and outright persecution have prevailed between them. But Romans 11 gives us helpful insights into how to live with Jewish friends and neighbors.

Twice in this passage Paul asks, "Did God reject his people?" And both times Paul answers, "By no means!" Is God through with Israel because of the crucifixion and resurrection of Christ? Because they turned a deaf ear to Jesus, has God rejected them?

Has he said they no longer have any place in his scheme of things? *No.* God is not through with the Jews.

Anyone who teaches that the church has inherited the promises of Israel should take a second look at the Scriptures, especially Romans 11. It is amazing how many apply to the church the blessings and glories promised to Israel in the Old Testament, but then unfairly apply all the cursings and the punishments to Israel!

Let's take a look at Paul's examination of this issue.

> *I ask then, Did God reject his people? By no means! I am an Israelite myself, a descendant of Abraham, from the tribe of Benjamin. God did not reject his people, whom he foreknew (11:1-2).*

Those among the Jews whom God foreknew, he did not reject. Paul is the great example of this. Here we have clear evidence that God has never set aside Jews with respect to individual salvation. Through the Christian centuries Jews have been coming to Christ, coming back to God, and coming into the fulfillment of the promise of Abraham by faith in Jesus Christ.

Notice that Paul refers to himself as one of those foreknown, one of the elect, one whom God has set aside to be his. In the letter to the Galatians the apostle reminds us this was done from his mother's womb, so that all through those years of resistance and pharisaical anger at the claims of Jesus, when Paul was persecuting the church and "breathing out threatenings and slaughters," he was nevertheless one of the elect. Though he was struggling, he was one whom God was inexorably drawing to himself. And Paul never forgot it. In many of his letters he marvels at the grace of God that took him—a blasphemer and persecutor of the church—and changed his heart, making him into a new creature in Christ. He is but one example of the many thousands of Jews through the centuries who have believed in Christ.

But even this does not exhaust the position of Israel in God's program. Not only do some Jews become Christian, but many who remain Jews may nevertheless be born-again, saved individuals. Paul cites an example from the prophet Elijah:

> *Don't you know what the Scripture says in the passage about Elijah—how he appealed to God against Israel: "Lord, they have killed your prophets and torn down your altars; I am the only one left, and they are trying to kill me"? And what was God's answer to him? "I have reserved for myself seven thousand who have not bowed the knee to Baal." So too, at the present time there is a remnant chosen by grace. And if by grace, then it is no longer by works; if it were, grace would no longer be grace (11:2-6).*

There was a time in the life of Elijah when he thought he was the only one left. This was after the tremendous encounter with the priests of Baal recorded in 1 Kings 18, when fire came down from heaven and consumed the sacrifices. Queen Jezebel mounted a persecution against the prophets of God, including Elijah, and brought Elijah to where he felt he was the only one left.

Broken Computer

Have you ever felt like that? "O Lord, they have all forsaken you. I'm the only one left. I'm the only one who's faithful." This was how Elijah felt. But God said, "Elijah, your computer is broken. You see only one left; I see seven thousand who have not bowed the knee to Baal. I have kept them from it. I have reserved to myself these seven thousand."

Like many of us, Elijah made mistakes. *First* he forgot about man's limited knowledge on any subject. We don't see very clearly; we don't understand all the issues. It is never as bad as it looks, no matter how bad it gets—and in these coming years it may get bad. But it will never be as bad as it looks, because our knowledge does not encompass the ones who remain faithful.

Second, Elijah forgot about God's unlimited power. The situation is never as bad as it looks because God is never as weak as he seems. Sometimes we think God must have lost the battle; the powers of darkness are so strong and violent that God must have given up. But when we think this way, we have forgotten what the Scriptures tell us again and again: God uses the very opposition of the enemy to bring about his purposes. Never forget this. God cannot lose because he uses the enemy's opposition to win. Elijah had no reason to despair.

Third, Elijah forgot about life's unmixable principles. If salvation is by grace, then it can't be by works. If it is by works, then it can't be by grace. Grace, you see, is God at work. Works is man at work. We often think we must earn our way to heaven. I find this even in the thinking of many Christians. A man said to me the other day, "Why should this happen to me? What have I done to deserve this kind of trial?" I realized I had said the same thing not long before. I really thought I had put God in my debt, and had somehow earned something better from him. That is works, and Paul reminds us here that you cannot mix works and grace. If God is going to call you and save you and deliver you, then it is not going to depend on your works. As James points out, your works will be there if your faith is real, because faith produces works. But the works do not save. This is what Elijah forgot.

So just as in Paul's day, thousands of Jews today have perhaps never really heard about Jesus. Many are earnest, devout, humble souls, trusting in the Old Testament record. They have never heard anything about Jesus to make them feel he really is their Messiah. And yet they have faithfully believed what the Old Testament reveals about the Messiah, the only bit of Christ they know. Are they not a part of this "remnant of grace"? Paul seems to suggest this.

Results of Unbelief

At any rate, Paul has made it clear God is not rejecting individuals out of Israel. Yet the majority of Jews are turning away.

> *What then? What Israel sought so earnestly it did not obtain, but the elect did. The others were hardened, as it is written:*
>
> *"God gave them a spirit of stupor,*
> *eyes so that they could not see*
> *and ears so that they could not hear,*
> *to this very day."*

And David says,

> *"May their table become a snare and a trap,*
> *a stumbling block and a retribution for them.*
> *May their eyes be darkened so they cannot see,*
> *and their backs be bent forever" (11:7-10).*

These are horrible words, but they are God's reaction to unbelief. When you hear truth, it is always important to do something about it. If you know something is true, you had better act on it. If you don't, you gradually lose your capacity to recognize truth. Dry rot will slowly set in, just as is described here, and now is visible among many in Israel today. Paul calls it a blindness. Even when the truth is there they cannot see it. Their ears are deaf. Even when loving appeals and warnings are set before them, they do not hear.

Their table, their food, becomes a snare and a trap leading into slavery. The food of Israel referred to here is the Law, the Scriptures. Jews highly value the Law, even though many don't know a lot about it. Many Jews today are hardly acquainted with anything in the Old Testament. The rabbis have given themselves to the study of it, and yet their study seems only to sink them deeper and deeper into the trap of legalistic slavery. They are bound by rituals and spend their days constantly working out interpretative details.

Odd Logic

Not long ago I read of an occasion when Nazi propaganda minister Joseph Goebbels said to a rabbi, "I understand you Jews have a peculiar way of reasoning when you study the Scriptures, and I want you to teach it to me."

The rabbi replied, "We have three questions we ask a boy before he begins this study. If he can answer them, we let him in. If he can't, he has no chance."

Goebbels said, "Ask them of me. What's the first question?"

"The first," said the rabbi, "is this: Two men fall down a chimney. One comes out clean and the other is dirty. Which one washes?"

Goebbels quickly replied, "Oh, that's easy. The dirty one washes, of course."

"Wrong. It is the clean one who washes."

"How do you reason that?"

"After they fall down the chimney they look at each other. The dirty one sees the clean one and thinks he's clean too; but the clean one sees the dirty one and thinks he also is dirty, so he washes."

"All right," Goebbels said. "That's strange logic, but give me the second question."

The rabbi continued: "Two men fall down a chimney. One comes out dirty, and the other clean. Which one washes?"

"That's the same question!"

"No it isn't," the rabbi said, "it's an entirely different question."

"Well," Goebbels ventured, "I think I can answer it. The clean one washes."

"Wrong," the rabbi said. "The dirty man holds up his hands and sees they are dirty. So he washes."

"And what's the third question?"

"Two men fall down a chimney . . ."

Goebbels interrupted: "But that's the same one!"

"No, it isn't," the rabbi replied, "it's entirely different! What's the answer?"

"I don't know," Goebbels admitted.

"Neither of them washes—because it is a ridiculous story to begin with! How could two men fall down a chimney and one come out dirty and the other clean?"

This kind of strange, penetrating, and yet difficult reasoning accounts for much of Jewish unbelief. In a paper printed and distributed by rabbis in which the differences between Christianity and Judaism are described, one rabbi writes,

Paul claimed that obedience to the Torah (the Law) could not guarantee salvation; rather, salvation was obtainable only through acceptance of and faith in Christ Jesus. To believe that a person could atone for his own sinful condition through any efforts on his own, as, for example, by obeying the laws of the Torah, was accordingly a delusion. But Paul eagerly announced that what man could not himself accomplish, namely salvation, could still be accomplished for him. Only God, however, was powerful enough to atone for man's sinfulness, and Paul held that the death of Christ Jesus was that act of divine atonement.

We Jews have rejected this Gentile Christian view. Judaism, as shaped by our rabbis in Palestine, conceived of the body as a gift of God, and to this day we regard the body as holy and wholesome, not as a prison from which to escape. Any inclination by man to commit a wrongdoing, we hold, resides not in his body but in his heart or mind. And this inclination can be overcome by a change of heart or mind. Thus man, by himself, does indeed possess the power to atone for his own misdeeds, and we Jews have, in our Torah, the guidance directing our hearts and minds to righteous living.

On this basis, the Jews say, they can win their way to acceptance with God without dealing with inbred sin and without considering the full teaching of Scripture. Paul says many have been rejected because of this.

Lost Forever?

Now Paul takes up the second question:

Again I ask, Did they stumble so as to fall beyond recovery? Not at all! (11:11).

If you have read the book of Acts, you know that wherever Paul went he began his ministry with Jews. Only when the Jews refused to hear did he turn to the Gentiles. In all these cities, the Gentiles were blessed and enriched by his ministry only because the Jews had refused it. Gentiles were allowed to believe and to become different people in order to make the Jews jealous.

We Christians ought to be so alive, so vital in our Christianity, so enthused and full of joy and love toward one another that every Jew we contact will say to himself, "Why do they have it and we don't? Why do they have a light on their faces, and joy and love in their hearts?" We Gentiles must hang our heads in shame and admit that through the centuries there has been very little in the church to attract Israel's jealousy. It has often been the other way around! But Paul says God intended the Gentiles to become so alive as to awaken the Jews to belief.

Paul's second argument is that Israel must ultimately return to God because worldwide blessing will come only when this happens.

But if their transgression means riches for the world, and their loss means riches for the Gentiles, how much greater riches will their fullness bring! I am talking to you Gentiles. Inasmuch as I am the apostle to the Gentiles, I make much of my ministry in the hope that I may somehow arouse my own people to envy and save some of them. For if their rejection is the reconciliation of the world, what will their acceptance be but life from the dead? (11:12-15).

At the 1974 Congress for World Evangelization in Lausanne, Switzerland, I was moved to see every nation on earth represented there. Each nation had in some way been penetrated by the gospel's riches—not material prosperity, but the riches of freedom, of the human spirit made free. Wherever the gospel is freely proclaimed, people are free. But where it is resisted or rejected or ignored, people drift into violence, anarchy, exploitation, and tyranny. This is because human freedom comes by means of the gospel. We in the Gentile world ought to give thanks to God for the riches that have come our way because of Israel's blindness.

But Paul's argument is this: If these riches have come because of the Jews' rejection, what will it be like for us when Israel comes again into its proper position? According to the prophets, the earth will then blossom like a rose, and there will be no more war, "nothing to hurt or destroy in all God's holy mountain." Israel is the key. This is why every Christian should keep his eye on this remarkable people, and see what is happening to them.

The First Handful

Paul's third argument is found in verse 16:

> *If the part of the dough offered as firstfruits is holy, then the whole batch is holy; if the root is holy, so are the branches.*

It would take a good Jew to really understand this. Paul is referring to the offerings and sacrifices in the tabernacle. For the offering of the firstfruits, a pile of dough was made up, and the priest would take a handful of it and present it to God. Paul's argument is that if this first handful was acceptable and holy before God, the rest of the dough would be too. The firstfruits here is Abraham, the father of the nation of Israel. Abraham was accepted before God; therefore his true descendants will also be accepted before him. They are not cut off from God or from his relationship with them; they are claimed by God. The God who made Abraham holy by his faith is also able to make his descendants holy, when they exercise the faith of Abraham.

Paul's fourth argument pictures an olive tree:

> *If some of the branches have been broken off, and you, though a wild olive shoot, have been grafted in among the others and now share in the nourishing sap from the olive root, do not boast over those branches. It you do, consider this: You do not support the root, but the root supports you. You will say then, "Branches were broken off so that I could be grafted in." Granted. But they were broken off because of unbelief, and you stand by faith. Do not be arrogant, but be afraid. For if God did not spare the natural branches, he will not spare you either (11-17-21).*

The olive tree, like the first handful of dough, symbolizes Abraham. The New Testament tells us a Gentile who becomes a Christian becomes also a son of Abraham. In a sense, he becomes an Israelite. But when a Jew becomes a Christian, he doesn't have to become a Gentile. The Jews are the *natural* fruit of the olive tree. We Gentiles are grafted in.

C. S. Lewis put it this way: "In a sense, the converted Jew is the only normal human being in the world. Everyone else is, from one point of view, a special case dealt with under emergency conditions." God opened the back door and let us Gentiles in as an emergency case. But those who really belong are the Jews. It is healthy for Gentile Christians to remember this. The Jews are not hanging around waiting for us to be nice to them. *They* have been nice to us. We ought to remember it, and respond with gratitude and humility to what God has done by placing us in this olive tree.

Paul's last argument is found in verses 22-24:

> *Consider therefore the kindness and sternness of God: sternness to those who fell, but kindness to you, provided that you continue in his kindness. Otherwise, you also will be cut off. And if they do not persist in unbelief, they will be grafted in, for God is able to graft them in again. After all, if you were cut out of an olive tree that is wild by nature, and contrary to nature were grafted into a cultivated olive tree, how much more readily will these, the natural branches, be grafted into their own olive tree!*

The olive tree signifies the faith of Abraham, the position of receiving blessing from the God of the earth through sheer grace, without any merit on his part. Paul says we who were like a wild olive tree, with hard, shriveled, bitter fruit, were taken and grafted into this rich olive tree. But this is contrary to what happens in nature.

If you take a nectarine branch and graft it into a peach tree, what does the branch produce from then on—peaches or nectarines? It still grows nectarines. The fruit is determined by the branch, not by the tree. The peach tree will grow nectarines on a nectarine branch, and plums on a plum branch, and so on. This is what happens according to nature. Following Paul's analogy here, if we, a wild olive branch, were grafted into a rich, cultivated olive tree, the fruit continuing to grow on the branch would be wild olives, bitter and shriveled.

But God does a miracle with us. He changes us so

the fruit coming forth is the fruit of the Spirit, and
we begin to produce the rich, wonderful, fat fruit of
the good olive tree in our lives. Again, Paul argues,
if God can do this with bitter fruit such as we Gentile
believers are, how much more will he produce with
the true branches?

How God Appears to You

Then Paul speaks of the kindness and the severity
of God. If you come to God needy and repentant, acknowledging your need for help, you will always find
him to be a loving, gracious, openhearted Sovereign,
ready to help you, ready to forgive you, ready to give
you all you need. But if you come to God complain-
ing, excusing yourself, justifying what you've been
doing and trying to make it look good in his sight,
you will always find God as hard as iron, as merciless
as fire, and as stern as a judge. God will invariably
turn a terrifying face toward those who come in pride
and self-justification.

This is the secret of the mystery of Israel's blindness today. As long as the Jews come to God in self-
justification they will always find a hard, iron-willed,
stern God. But as Zechariah the prophet describes,
when Jesus appears and they look on him whom they
had pierced, they will ask him, "Where did you get
those wounds in your hands?" He will say, "These I
received in the house of my friends." Then they will
mourn for him as one mourns for an only child, and
the mourning of Israel that day will be like the
mourning for Hadad Rimmon in the plains of
Megiddo. The whole nation will mourn. Then God
will take this nation and bless them, and they will
replenish the earth.

This is surely a reminder to our own hearts of the
faithfulness of God. His promises will not fail. God's
purposes will never be shortchanged. God is going to

accomplish all he says he will do. Though it may be the long way around, and lead through many trials, temptations, hurts and heartaches, what God has said he will do. He will carry it through.

6
OUR GREAT AND GLORIOUS GOD

(Romans 11:25—12:1)

In the closing verses of chapter 11 Paul prophesies the restoration of Israel. Up to now he has been arguing this from reason, but now he prophesies the restoration directly:

> I do not want you to be ignorant of this mystery, brothers, so that you may not be conceited: Israel has experienced a hardening in part until the full number of the Gentiles has come in. And so all Israel will be saved, as it is written:
>
> The deliverer will come from Zion;
> he will turn godlessness away from Jacob.

> *And this is my covenant with them*
> *when I take away their sins."*
>
> *As far as the gospel is concerned, they are enemies*
> *on your account; but as far as election is con-*
> *cerned, they are loved on account of the pa-*
> *triarchs, for God's gifts and his call are irrevo-*
> *cable (11:25-29).*

Perhaps the most striking thing about this passage
is that Paul calls the Jews' present resistance to the
gospel a "mystery." He does not mean it is obscure
and difficult to understand. The word *mystery* in
Scripture refers to something supernatural, not
brought about by natural causes.

If you have ever witnessed to a Jew, perhaps you
have run up against what seemed to be a rock wall of
indifference to your message. This resistance may
well have been what Paul is talking about here, a
strange hardening toward the gospel on the part of
the Jews. This hardening, which Paul calls a mystery, cannot be explained by normal reasons. He says
three things about this, and we must take care to
notice them.

First, it is a hardening "in part." Not all Jews are
afflicted this way. We are not told how many in Israel
are going to be hardened. All we are told is that some
Jews will not listen to and receive the gospel. No one
can say any given person is a part of this hardening.
But we can say the Jews will exhibit (as has been evident in history) a strange and remarkable resistance
to the gospel.

This hardening is also limited in duration: "until
the full number of the Gentiles comes in." Jews are
not bound to experience hardening forever. What
does "the full number of the Gentiles" mean? The

word the apostle uses here means literally "the fullness" of the Gentiles. What does this "fullness" mean?

Some interpret it to mean a certain number of Gentiles will be converted. God has a precise number in mind and he is going to let the gospel go out to all the world until that number of Gentiles has been converted. Then he will release Israel from its blindness, its hardness. But I do not think Paul is referring to a number.

This is the second time in chapter 11 the word "fullness" is used. The first time it was used not of the Gentiles, but of the Jews. In verse 12 Paul says of Israel, "But if their transgression means riches for the world, and their loss means riches for the Gentiles, how much greater riches will their *fullness* bring!" Here is the same word, *pleroma,* which means "that which fills." Notice it is set in direct contrast to the words "their loss" or "their fall." This "fall" refers to the time when Israel was driven out of Jerusalem by Roman armies in A.D. 70 and scattered throughout all the nations of the earth.

Restored Spiritual Riches

This loss does not mean a diminished number of Jews. The Jews have increased in number throughout these centuries of dispersion. Paul is talking rather about diminished spiritual riches. The Jews have lost the quality and richness of their relationship with God. Though they have the Law and the outward trappings of faith, still they have lost the richness of relationship that sets the heart aglow and the face radiant with the light, love, beauty, grace, and character of God. This is the loss; therefore "the fullness" means the restoration of these riches. So when Paul speaks of "the fullness of the Gentiles," he is describing a Gentile church so spiritually rich it will awaken Israel's envy.

Anyone who reads church history knows the Gentile churches have not had much vitality to awaken the Jews to envy! The Jews see mostly enemies among Gentile Christians. Often the Jews have been oppressed, persecuted, and terribly treated by those professing to be Christians. But Paul is saying a very hopeful thing here: A day is coming when Gentile churches will be enriched with such spiritual blessing that the Jews will say, "We should have that! That's the way we could be!" Then the Jews will be open as never before to the gospel of the grace of God.

Perhaps we are seeing a taste of this now. This is one reason why Jews, in greater number than since the time of the dispersion, have been open to the gospel and turning to Christ. It is is an amazing and encouraging thing. This is what the apostle says must take place.

Paul says the prophets told us this would happen: "The deliverer will come from Zion; he will turn godlessness away from Jacob." This is the promise of the Old Testament. Furthermore, quoting from Jeremiah, he says, "And this is my covenant with them when I take away their sins." The Deliverer is coming and forgiveness will be granted to Israel. The prophets make it clear. So the apostle closes with two important things we ought to remember about the Jews: "As far as the gospel is concerned, they are enemies on your account; but as far as election is concerned, they are loved on account of the patriarchs, for God's gifts and his call are irrevocable" (11:28-29).

The Jews may treat a Gentile Christian as an enemy due to this strange, supernatural hardening of part of Israel. This has been the experience of many who have gone as missionaries to the Jews. They have been treated as though they were attacking the Jews instead of trying to minister to them and help them. They have aroused the enmity and anger of the Jews. I have heard the group called "Jews for Jesus" tell of meeting violence and personal attack when they go into Jewish communities to talk about their experience as Jews who have found the glory and grace of God in Jesus Christ.

Any such missionary movement among the Jews seems to create extreme resentment and consternation in Jewish ranks. As you witness to Jews, it is well to remember you may be treated as an enemy. But remember also that the Jews are loved by an unchanging God who loves every Jew, without exception. No matter how stubborn or resistant they may be, he has set his love upon them, and the nations of the world had better not forget it! God has chosen the Jews.

Bound to Disobedience

The apostle now moves on to show us God's principle of salvation for all men:

> *Just as you who were at one time disobedient to God have now received mercy as a result of their disobedience, so they too have now become disobedient in order that they too may now receive mercy as a result of God's mercy to you. For God has bound all men over to disobedience so that he may have mercy on them all (11:30-32).*

In this striking statement we see something of how the mind of God works, and the strange wheels-within-wheels with which he moves in history to bring about his purposes. Paul declares that God used the Jews' disobedience, their rejection of their own Messiah, to allow rebellious Gentiles to receive mercy and grace from his hand. It was only by the Jews' disobedience that the gospel went out to the Gentiles.

This answers again the question with which this whole section begins. In Romans 9 Paul asks, "Has God failed?" Since God obviously has been trying to reach the Jews, even sending his own Son as their Messiah (whom they rejected), does it mean God has failed? The answer is now clear. No, God has not failed. He used Jewish rejection to reach the Gentile world, which he had intended to reach all along. This was his way of bringing it about.

Then, after having shown mercy to the Gentiles, God now uses the very mercies he has shown to the Gentiles to make the Jews angry and rebellious so they too can receive mercy. Paul says unless one realizes how rebellious his heart is, he has no chance to receive mercy. Thus God works in human history to make us aware of our basic, inherent rebellion against him. Paul concludes that everyone is a rebel, and God wants all people to admit it so they can receive mercy.

What keeps any individual or nation from receiving God's mercy? It is a self-righteous, self-confident attitude of "I don't need help. I can handle it myself. I am able to solve all the problems of life on my own. I don't need God." Anyone with this attitude has cut himself off from God's mercy, without which we can never become fully human. So God, as Paul puts it here, has "bound all men over to [the knowledge of their] disobedience so that he may have mercy on them all."

The Deep Riches

This reminder of the strange ways in which God works awakens in the apostle's heart an outburst of praise and adoration:

> *Oh, the depth of the riches of the wisdom and*
> *knowledge of God!*
> *How unsearchable his judgments,*
> *and his paths beyond tracing out!*
> *"Who has known the mind of the Lord?*
> *Or who has been his counselor?"*
> *"Who has ever given to God,*
> *that God should repay him?"*
> *For from him and through him and to him*
> *are all things.*
> *To him be the glory forever! Amen*
> *(11:33-36).*

Paul's heart has been stirred by what he calls the deep riches of God's wisdom and his ways. They are beyond human exploration. There is no way we can finally fathom God.

God is greater than man. He is ever beyond us, and we must always remember that. Our minds cannot grasp his greatness. We can understand what he tells us about himself, but beyond this there is much more we cannot know. There are depths of riches. This is why we are always being surprised by God. He is forever enriching us in ways we do not anticipate.

Then Paul speaks of God's "unsearchable judgments." These are "acts of God," such as droughts, which totally mystify the meteorologists, or earthquakes. Often we are baffled when these things occur. But God's ways are unsearchable. No man can

call God to account and say, "You have no right to do
that!" Though we attempt this all the time, we have
no right to do it. For God is beyond us; he knows in-
finitely more than we do.

Paul is then impressed by the untraceable ways of
God, the paths of God beyond understanding. We
can't put them all together. We can believe them,
but we can't explain them. For instance, it is clear
from Scripture that nothing God has planned ever interferes with human responsibility. Nothing God has
said will in any way infringe on our free will. We are
free to make choices. We know it. We feel ourselves
free to decide to do this or that, to do good or bad.
Nothing God plans interferes with this freedom of
human choice. And yet nothing we do can ever frus-
trate God's sovereign plan. Whatever we choose with
the freedom of choice we have, ultimately it all works
out to accomplish what God has determined shall be
done. This is the kind of God we have. Little wonder
Paul bows in worship!

Searching Questions

God's inscrutable wisdom and ways are contrasted
with the impotence of man. Paul asks three searching
questions. If you have trouble with God's wisdom,
try to answer his questions. The first one is, "Who
has known the mind of the Lord?" Who has ever anticipated what God is going to do? Have you? Have
you ever been able to figure out how God is going to
handle the situations you get into? We all try, but it
never turns out quite the way we think it will. There
is always a little twist to it we never could have
guessed.

We see this in the case of Jesus. The Pharisees
asked him, "Should we pay taxes to Caesar?" They

thought they had him. If he said no, the Romans would be angry at him; if he said yes, the Jews would be angry at him. Do you remember how he handled it? He called for a coin and said, "Whose picture is on this coin?" They answered, "Caesar's." He said, "All right. What Caesar has put his image on, give to Caesar (that is, pay your taxes); but what God has put his image on, give to him." God has put his image on men. This is what they owed God—themselves. The Pharisees couldn't handle such an answer. It devastated them.

Remember the woman caught in adultery? Her self-righteous accusers were ready to put her to death. When they brought her to Jesus, he just stooped and wrote on the ground. He looked up, finally, and said, "He that is without sin among you, let him cast the first stone." They stood there puzzled, then every one of them began to think of other places they ought to be. Soon they were all gone, and no one was left except the woman and Jesus. How could you have anticipated the way he handled this? How unsearchable are his judgments! Who has anticipated what God is going to do? No one.

Second question: "Or who has been his counselor?" Who has ever suggested something God had never thought of? Have you ever tried it? I have. I have sometimes looked at a situation and saw a way to work it all out and suggested it to God. I thought I had been very helpful to him. But in the final outworking of the matter, it turned out he knew things I didn't know and he was working out things I never saw and could not have seen. God's final outworking was right, and mine would have been wrong.

Paul's last question is, "Who has ever given to God, that God should repay him?" Who has put God in his debt? Paul reminds us that everything we are and have comes from him. He gives to us; we don't give to him. There is *nothing* we could give to God that he doesn't already own or have in abundance, or couldn't make if he had to! So Paul concludes with this great outburst: "For from him and through him and to him are all things. To him be the glory forever! Amen."

God is the *originator* of all things; all things come from him. He is the *sustainer* of all things; they all depend of him. As C. S. Lewis puts it, "To argue with God is to argue with the very power that makes it possible to argue at all!" He is the end purpose of all. All things find their culmination in God. He is the *reason* why all things exist. Therefore, "to him be the glory forever! Amen!"

Then in Romans 12:1 (this break between chapters 11 and 12 must be the worst chapter division in the entire Bible) Paul goes right on to say,

> *Therefore {because God is like this and you are like that}, I urge you, brothers, in view of God's mercy, to offer your bodies as living sacrifices, holy and pleasing to God—which is your spiritual worship (12:1).*

"Spiritual worship" in the Greek here is literally "logical service." It is only logical and reasonable for man to be available to God. This is the logical reason for our existence. "Therefore," he says, "bring your bodies." If you are a Christian, your spirit has already been surrendered to God. But you are trying to live a split life, a schizophrenic life, if your body does not follow what your spirit has already done. Now put your body where your mouth is and follow through with what your spirit has said to God. Be his available instrument.

What Paul describes here is not an act of the moment, but a commitment for the rest of your life. You are to make your body available to God for as long as you live. Paul does not talk about your soul or your spirit because in this life you can never do anything without your body. If the body is available, the soul and spirit accompany it. So put your body on the line. Bring it as a living sacrifice, and the God of greatness and glory and of infinite riches and wisdom and power will fill it with his own amazing presence, and you will never find life the same again.

7
LIVING DAY
BY DAY

(Romans 12:1-2)

Let's take a closer look now at the opening verse of
Romans 12, which is the conclusion of Paul's argument in chapter 11. Because God is rich and wise and
great and glorious, and a God of love and mercy—
while we are ignorant of the future, forgetful of the
past, unable to control the present—the apostle says,

> *Therefore, I urge you, brothers, in view of God's*
> *mercy, to offer your bodies as living sacrifices,*
> *holy and pleasing to God—which is your*
> *spiritual worship. Do not conform any longer to*
> *the pattern of this world, but be transformed by*
> *the renewing of your mind. Then you will be able*

*to test and approve what God's will is—his
good, pleasing and perfect will (12:1-2).*

These are familiar words. You have read them
many times. The Jerusalem Bible translates the first
sentence,

*Think of God's mercies, my brothers, and wor-
ship him, I beg you, in a way that is worthy—by
offering him your living bodies.*

This is what we sing in the closing words of the
great hymn, "When I Survey the Wondrous Cross":

*Love so amazing, so divine,
Demands my soul, my life, my all.*

When Paul says to "present your bodies," he uses a
tense that means it is something we do once for all,
rather than over and over again. Do it once, and then
live the rest of your life on that basis. There comes a
time in a Christian's life when God wants you to
bring your body to him, recognizing for the rest of
your life his right to use your body for his purposes.

Source of the Trouble

It amazes me that God would ever want our
bodies. You may ask, "Why would he want my
body? I can hardly stand it myself at times." But God
says, "Bring your body." Paul has been talking about
the body all the way through this section of Romans.
He tells us the body is the seat of what he calls "the
flesh," the antagonistic nature within us that does not
like what God likes and does not want to do what
God wants. We all have it, and somehow it is located
in or connected with the body. Your body is the
source of temptation. That God would want this
body is unbelievable, and yet he does.

Some of us perhaps are saying, "Lord, surely you don't want this body. Let me tell you about it. It has B.O.! It snores! It has a bad heart. It has a dirty mind. You don't want this body, Lord. I have such trouble with it. It is always tripping me up. My spirit is great, and I worship you with my soul—but the body, Lord, that's what gets me down!"

But the Lord says, "Bring your body. I know all about it. I know more about it than you do. I know all the things you tell me about it plus some things you haven't learned yet. By means of the blood of Jesus, and by the work of the Holy Spirit, I have made it (as Paul wrote) *holy and pleasing.*"

This is the beautiful appeal of these words. Paul is not telling us we must get cleaned up and get our lives straightened out and become perfect before we can offer ourselves to God. No, Paul says, "I urge you, brothers and sisters, in view of God's mercy, to offer yourselves as living sacrifices. Bring your bodies as living sacrifices unto God." Bring your body with all its problems, with all its temptations—bring it just the way it is!

I don't know how this affects you, but it encourages me greatly. All other religions tell us we must clean up our lives first, and then offer them to God. God never talks that way. He says, "Come to me just the way you are. I am the answer to your problems; therefore, start with me. You can't handle those problems yourself. Don't start with the idea that you have to straighten them out. Come to me, because I have the answers."

Week-long Worship

Furthermore, Paul tells us, this is the only thing that makes sense. "This is your logical worship."

This is the way to worship God. I hear many people speaking on worship these days. When you come to a church you come to worship corporately, together. But worship does not start or end in church. You are worshiping or you are not worshiping all week long, depending on what you do with your body. Is it God's? Is it his to use right where you are—at work, in your home, with your family? Worship is allowing God to use your body to be the dynamic through which he works in every situation. This is your logical worship, the only thing that makes sense.

If you use your body for yourself, you will misuse it, abuse it. You will use it for things the body was never intended to be used for. Or you will destroy or hurt it. We know this is true. You will either ruin it, or you will spend so much time preserving it, pouring lotions on it, exposing it to the sun, and all the other things people do, that you never get around to using it for what God has intended. But if you give your body to God, he will use it rightly. "So give it to me," God says, "and I will use it wherever you go to bring peace, to give joy, to heal hurt, and to show love, healing, and grace. I will bless the world through your body." The only logical, sensible thing to do with your body is to bring it to the Lord just as it is, without any attempt to improve it, and say, "Lord, here it is. Take me, Lord, and begin to use me."

"Well, this sounds great," you say, "but how do I do it? How does it work?" The Lord says, "Once you bring your body to me, I will take it. But you need to keep doing two things. First, do not conform any longer to the pattern of this world. Second, be transformed by the renewing of your mind. Then you will be able to test and approve what God's will is—his good, pleasing, and perfect will." These two commands are both in the present tense, meaning they are things you keep on doing. You bring your body once—you give it to God and live the rest of your life on that commitment—and then do these two things every day.

Sell Your TV?

The first of these commands, "Do not be conformed to the pattern of this world," refers literally to "the schemes of this world," the schemes men come up with to regulate and run their lives. The Word of the Lord is, "Stop being conformed to that." "Oh," you say, "I know exactly what you are talking about. It means don't smoke or drink or play cards, and if you're really spiritual, sell your television set and never drink coffee or tea again."

I grew up thinking that way. There was always a list of forbidden activities. Many other things the world did were not on the list, but the things mentioned above were usually on it. I had to learn, through rather painful experience, that those things are neither good nor bad in themselves. I know people who have given up all of them and yet are still saturated by the spirit of the age—which is what the word *world* here really means; the pattern and spirit of this age, the philosophy of life surrounding us.

The spirit of the age is always the same. It never changes from generation to generation. The basis of it is clearly the advancement of self. Everyone in the world lives to advance himself. "What do I get out of this? What's in it for me?" But God says to us, "Don't be locked into this kind of thinking, because it brings heartache and ruin and disaster into your life. Don't live on this basis anymore. Don't get caught up with this kind of thinking. It's wrong! It is twisted and distorted, and it won't work. Don't be trapped by it."

The spirit of the age is to seek my personal happiness. If the advancement of self is the basis for all life, then the goal of all life is personal happiness. You hear this on every side. Unfortunately it has infiltrated the church as well. Christians talk this way as much as anyone. They say, "The reason I work and live is to have my needs met, my desires fulfilled." I hear people saying, "I'm thinking of leaving this church and going to another one, because this one doesn't meet my needs," as though the only reason for ever going to church is to have your needs met! This is the thinking of the world, the spirit of the age. To think this way is to be conformed to the world, regardless of whether one drinks or smokes or chews or plays cards.

The spirit of the age includes also the methods of the world. You have only to look around to see what these are: rivalry and competition, getting ahead of the other guy, grabbing what's mine before someone else gets it, hanging onto everything I've got no matter what it costs in terms of hurt or pain to someone else. The pressure to conform to these methods pervades all society. Around us the whole climate of life is squeezing us, insisting that we conform and making it costly if we don't. But God says, "Don't let the world around you pressure you into thinking this way any longer."

Response to Stardom

The life of opera singer Jerome Hines illustrates what it means to refuse to be conformed to the world. As a trained and talented musician he became possessed with a desire to become a star in the Metropolitan Opera Company. This was what he lived for. He gave up all other activities, all other pursuits, all other pleasures, to give himself to the necessary work of training to become an opera star. Perfecting the arts of intonation, of musical projection, he learned several languages so he could sing operatic roles. He gave himself over to his desire to be a star. Finally it came true. He became a star. And he said it was empty, hollow. One day he heard a man singing. The voice was as good as his, and the man could have done what he did. It was George Beverly Shea singing, "I'd Rather Have Jesus." The words he sang were,

> *I'd rather have Jesus than silver or gold,*
> *I'd rather be His than have riches untold,*
> *I'd rather have Jesus than houses or lands,*
> *I'd rather be led by His nail-pierced hands*
> *Than to be the king of a vast domain*
> *And be held in sin's dread sway.*
> *I'd rather have Jesus than anything*
> *This world affords today.*

This song greatly moved Jerome Hines. He began to think about his life, and became a Christian. But he didn't quit the opera. Many people thought he should have. They thought the opera was "worldly." No, opera is not worldly—except to those in opera who think like worldlings and live like worldlings. Jerome Hines stayed in opera, but everything was different. He was no longer singing for the advancement of Jerome Hines, but for the glory of God. He dedicated his art, his work, his all to this new purpose.

Then Hines had an opportunity to sing the role he had always wanted to sing and had trained for through months and months of hard work. He was given a contract that stated he was to sing this role in the opera for ten years.

But one day when he went to the opera house to practice for it, he found some people performing a rather lewd dance and was told, "This is the choreography introducing the opera." He said, "There's nothing in the opera like this!" "No," they said, "we're changing it a bit, modernizing it, bringing it up to date." Jerome Hines said, "I won't sing if you are going to have this kind of dance in it." He was told he had better go talk to Mr. Bing.

Hines went to Rudolph Bing, general manager of the Metropolitan Opera, and said to him "Sir, if you have that dance in the opera I am not going to sing in it." Bing told him, "If you don't sing, you will be ostracized and blacklisted in opera. You are under contract to sing." Hines said, "Sir, I can't sing in that opera. I am not going to let my name be used to entice people to come in to see filth like this. You can break me, sir, and the union can break me. I've worked hard for months to train for this role, but I will not sing in your opera if that dance is in it."

Bing said, "Jerome, you don't have to sing. If you really feel this way, we'll get someone else. But we can't change the contract." So Hines gave up the role. It cost him, over the period of ten years, something like a hundred thousand dollars.

How many of us are willing to give our bodies to God to the extent of giving up a hundred thousand dollars rather than do something offensive to the Lord? This is what Paul means by not being conformed to this world—not going along with its pattern of thinking, not being willing to go in for all it seeks in its pursuit of pleasure and happiness. "That's tough," you say. You bet it's tough! If you do it day after day it's very hard, because you are under constant pressure and it gets to you after a while: Everyone else is thinking and acting the world's way, and no one understands you—so why not give in?

Thinking with the Mind of Christ

That question has only one answer. To stand up against this kind of pressure you need what Paul talks about next: "Be transformed by the renewing of your mind." There is no way you can keep from being conformed to the world unless you are being transformed by the renewing of your mind. Something has to happen to your thinking. You can't go on thinking the way the world around you thinks and not give in and be conformed to what it does. What we need is a change of thinking, a change that comes day by day by being renewed again and again and again. You need a mind that will see through all the silly schemes of the world. In the Scriptures this kind of mind is called "the mind of Christ." The mind of Christ is to look at life as Jesus does, seeing life as he sees it. It is seeing what is really there and not what seems to be there, seeing what really is important, not what appears to be important. You can't have this mind unless your mind is being renewed every day.

The mind of Christ says the reason for living is not to advance self, but to serve God and advance his will. Not your will, but his will be done; not the building of your kingdom and your empire, but the advancement of his kingdom. This is really what human beings are here for, and to maintain this kind of thinking in the midst of the world takes a renewed mind.

A young businessman once told me he made a list of all the reasons for working at his company: the salary, the benefits, the prestige and status, the opportunity to rub shoulders with men who could help him in his profession, the opportunity to be involved in work in which he found intense pleasure.

When he finished the list, he looked at it and said to himself, "That's just a human list—the things anybody would put down. But I'm a Christian. I ought to have other reasons for being here." So on another piece of paper he began to list all the reasons he believed *God* wanted him there. He began to see things he hadn't thought much about before. He listed names of many of the people he occasionally was able to help by offering Christian insights to aid in their personal and emotional needs. He thought of the fellow at the desk next to his who especially needed his help. He thought of opportunities he had to bring a witness to his whole company. When he finished, he realized these were the real reasons he was in his job. His salary and advancement were really quite trivial; the enduring thing, the thing that would last forever, was not what he got out of it, but what God got out of it.

This is what this passage is talking about—renewing your mind so you see your life as God sees it. The mind of Christ realizes life's goal is not to please yourself but to please God. And the way you please God is to depend on him to work through you, where you are; to believe he has the power and the wisdom and the strength to do things in ways you can't anticipate or even dream of. God is pleased when people venture out in faith.

Settlers and Pioneers

Wes Seeliger has described the two kinds of theology in Christian life today in terms of the Old West. One outlook he called "Settler Theology" and the other "Pioneer Theology." In Settler Theology the church is the courthouse in the center of a little town. In Pioneer Theology the church is a covered wagon, out on the trail, never stopping, involved in battles and bearing the scars of many fights, getting stuck in the mud and being pulled out again.

In Settler Theology, God is the mayor. He lives up on the top floor of the courthouse and keeps an eagle eye on everything going on in town. In Pioneer Theology, God is the trail boss, rough and rugged and tough and hardhitting; he won't let anyone stop—he keeps them going. He gets down shoulder to the wheel when they get stuck in the mud.

In Settler Theology, Jesus is the sheriff. He wears a white hat and goes around plugging all the bad boys who come into town. He determines who goes to jail and who doesn't. In Pioneer Theology, Jesus is the scout ahead of the party, exposed to all the dangers of the trail, finding out where the wagon is to go next. He is the pioneer's pioneer.

In Settler Theology the Holy Spirit is the saloon girl. She keeps everyone comforted and happy. In Pioneer Theology the Holy Spirit is the buffalo hunter who provides daily meat for the wagon train. He amuses himself by going up to the courthouse window every Sunday, when all the settlers are having an ice cream party, and firing off a tremendous blast from his shotgun, scaring the living daylights out of all the people inside.

In Settler Theology the preacher is the banker. He keeps all the resources in town under control. Everything has to go through him. In Pioneer Theology the preacher is the cook. He dishes out the food the buffalo hunter provides. He's no better than any of the other pioneers; he just keeps them fed.

This irreverent but accurate overview presents a good lesson on New Testament Christianity:

Christians are not sent into the world to build their own little nests, to feather them and keep them nice and comfortable, and to try to get by without being polluted by the things around them. Jesus said we are to go into the world like sheep in the midst of wolves. We are exposed to danger and pressure and trouble and battle all the time. The only thing keeping us from succumbing to this subversive propaganda all around us is to continually have our minds renewed by the Word of God.

In Line with God's Word

How do you get your mind renewed? One place is at church, wherever the Scriptures are taught, so you hear once again what the truth is—not what everyone in the world says is true. Your mind is also renewed in your personal Bible study. When you are confused and don't know where to go, you renew your mind by reading and thinking through the Scriptures, letting them speak to your heart so you can keep your life in line with God's Word. Your mind is also renewed in prayer and by spiritual fellowship with other believers. These are all part of the process of having a renewed mind.

What are you going to do with your life? Are you going to wrap it up in a napkin of affluence and bury it in forty years of self-indulgence? That would be the emptiest experience you could have. When you came before God's throne, you would find you simply wasted all those years.

Are you willing to bring your body to God and say, "Lord, here it is. I have trouble with it, and I'm sure you will too, but here it is. You wanted it. I give it to you for the rest of my life, to be your instrument for whatever you want"? And God says, "All right, I'll take it." If you come on this basis, beginning to recognize the systematic brainwashing of the world and refusing it, and constantly renewing your thinking in the truth as it is found in Jesus and the Word of God, then I will tell you something: You are going to have an exciting life, beyond anything you ever dreamed. It will never be dull. It will be terribly difficult sometimes, but never dull, never boring.

Many years ago a man was walking through Union Station in Chicago. It was busy and crowded. He had been thinking of what he might do with his life. It suddenly dawned on him the only logical thing he could do with his life, since it belonged to God and had been redeemed by the Lord, was to give it to him and ask him to use it. Right in the midst of the crowd he stopped and drew a little mark with his toe. Then he stood on the mark and said, "Lord, here I am, I am yours. The rest of my life, whatever you want me to do, if you will show me and convince me what you want, I will do it. The attitudes you want me to have, I will have. As I study and read your Word, I will try to carry out what you tell me to do, and think the way you tell me to think. Here I am, Lord; do with my life as you want." That commitment service in Union Station in Chicago was known only by this man and God. But God picked that man up and began to use him in remarkable ways. He has traveled the world and touched hundreds of lives because God used him.

If you want to stand where you are now and draw a little mark on the floor with your toe, that's fine. Give yourself to God, if it's what you want. He doesn't make anyone do it. That is why Paul puts it in these terms: "I beseech you, brothers; I beg you. It is the logical outcome of your life, the only thing making sense." Will you give yourself to him, so you can never forget you did it right here and right now?

Every time you come back to this spot you will think about it. "This is where I gave myself to God. This is where I said he had a right to use me. For the rest of my life, he can use my body and all that I am."

8
WHO AM I, LORD?

(Romans 12:3-8)

Be transformed by having your mind renewed! This is the secret Paul reveals. From verse 3 through the rest of chapter 12 the apostle explains specifically what it means to have your thinking changed.

The place to start is with yourself. God always starts there. He never seeks to use you to change others until he has changed you. Jesus said, "First remove the beam in your own eye, then you will see clearly how to help your brother remove the little sliver in his eye." This order is so important!

In verses 3-8 the apostle describes two areas involved in our thinking about ourselves: *who we are* and *what we have*. Let's begin with his word about who we are:

> *For by the grace given to me I say to every one of you: Do not think of yourself more highly than you ought, but rather think of yourself with sober judgment, in accordance with the measure of faith God has given you (12:3).*

First, says Paul, think about yourself. Many have the idea that the Christian life means never thinking about yourself, since we know ultimately we are to reach out to others. Others are forever going around taking their spiritual temperature and feeling their spiritual pulse, so that all they ever think about is themselves.

It is true the Scriptures tell you to examine yourself, to see whether you are in the faith or not, "to see whether Christ be in you," as Paul writes to the Corinthians. But it is wrong to think continually of nothing but yourself. Nevertheless, it is quite right to take time occasionally to evaluate where you are in your Christian experience. In fact, Paul exhorts us to do so with apostolic authority—"by the grace given to me" (that is, the gift of apostleship); on the basis of this office he exhorts every one of us to take time to think through who we are and what is going on in our lives.

Avoid Overrating

Paul stresses that you must do this in a way that avoids overrating yourself. "Do not think of yourself more highly than you ought." Doubtless he puts this first because it is such a natural tendency. Our flesh, our inherited Adamic nature, loves to think very highly of itself. Perhaps you have at times suddenly realized that your view of yourself is much higher than other people's view of you. This is often why we get upset with people—because they don't agree with our opinion about ourselves.

People can express an exalted self-view in two ways. We are familiar with the loud-mouthed braggart who goes around taking every occasion to tell you how smart he is, how much he's done, how capable he is, how much he can do if you just give him a chance. But others realize that people don't like braggarts, so they revert to the opposite form of the same problem. They deplore themselves, and talk about themselves as though they are nothing or no one. But this is merely another form of pride.

The reason you do this (I know, because I've done it myself) is that you hope others will correct you. You tell people all these bad things about yourself expecting them to say, "No, no, you're not like that at all!" And you say to yourself, "Come on, keep it up. Tell me more! Talk me out of this!" Of course, the way to make the true motive clear when people downplay themselves is simply to agree with them. Just say, "Well, I have to admit you are right," and watch the reaction. He'll be very upset with you, because you have offended his pride. His words were really only a pretense to humility. Paul says to avoid either one of these approaches.

The proper way to think about yourself is to observe the limits God has given. "Do not think . . . more highly than you ought (to think)." There is an "oughtness" to this matter of thinking about yourself. What is this "oughtness"? Negatively, the Scriptures suggest we ought not to judge ourselves by paying attention to our feelings. I am amazed at how many people determine what they are like or are able to do by the way they happen to feel at the moment. They trust their feelings, as though feelings give adequate and trustworthy information about themselves. But feelings can change and fluctuate a dozen times a minute. They are dependent upon many factors over which we have no control—whether our glands are working properly, whether the sun is shining, whether we ate too much, whether we got enough sleep—all these factors affect our feelings. Therefore the most foolish thing in the world is to judge yourself on the basis of how you feel at any given moment.

Feelings are important, and I don't mean to rule them out entirely. Sometimes Christians think feelings are all wrong. No, feelings are not wrong; they just should not be the basis for evaluating yourself.

On what basis, then, should you evaluate yourself? The answer, of course, is on how God sees you. This is reality—what God says you are. This is the realistic way to think about yourself. It is a twofold evaluation.

Something to Watch

First, Paul says, do not think of yourself more highly than you ought, "but think of yourself with sober judgment." So first, think soberly about yourself. What does this mean? What will sober you? Surely it refers to the teaching of the Scriptures on the Fall. We are all fallen creatures. All of us have within us this Adamic nature which is not to be trusted. As long as we are in the flesh, in the body, we are going to have this nature. So the first thing to remember about yourself is that something within you can never be trusted, and will always have to be watched. You'll have distorted thoughts and attitudes and temptations. So first of all, think soberly about yourself.

Second, think "with the measure of faith that God

has given you." Look back over all God has told you about what has happened since you have come to Christ. The degree to which you accept what God has said about you will give you confidence and courage and ability to function at any given task. You have this courage and ability according to how much you believe of what God has said.

And what has God said about you? Look back over the wonderful message of the first eight chapters of Romans: We are no longer in Adam, in our spirit, but are now united to Christ. He lives within us. His power is available to us. The Holy Spirit has come to enable us to say no to all the evil forces and temptations we come up against, so that sin shall not have dominion over us; for we are not under the law but under grace. This is the way to think about yourself. Remember to always be on guard because of the evil of the flesh within you. But you can always win because of the grace of God and the righteousness of Jesus Christ and the gift of the Holy Spirit.

When I get up in the morning I try to remind myself of three things: First, I am made in the image of God. I am not an animal and I don't have to behave like an animal. I have an ability within me, given to me by God himself, to respond and relate to God. Therefore I can behave as a man and not as a beast.

Second, I am filled with the Spirit of God. The most amazing thing has happened! Though I don't deserve it in the least degree, I have the power of God at work within me. I have become, in some sense, the bearer of God, and God himself is willing to be at work in me through the problems and pressures I will go through this day.

Third, I am part of the plan of God. God is working out all things to a great and final purpose in the earth, and I am part of it. What I do today has purpose and significance and meaning. This is not a meaningless day I am going through. Even the smallest incident, the most apparently insignificant word or relationship, is involved in his great plan. Therefore all of it has meaning and purpose.

I know of nothing better than these three thoughts to set me on my feet. They give me confidence without conceit. I have a sense of being able to cope, of being able to handle life. I know I don't deserve this gift of worth and grace, and yet I have it. Therefore I can't be conceited about it, but I can be confident in it.

In Front of the Mirror

Paul moves now to our life in the church, and takes up the subject of God's gifts. Not only are you who you are because of the work of Christ, but you also have what you have because of his work. Here the apostle says,

> *Just as each of us has one body with many members, and these members do not all have the same function, so in Christ we who are many form one body, and each member belongs to all the others (12:4).*

This is a beautiful picture of the church. Whatever your mental idea of what the church ought to be, God tells us his church is like a human body. If you want a good course in ecclesiology, just stand in front of your mirror some morning without your clothes on and examine your body. This is what the church is like.

Just as you have only one body and not two, so also there is only one church in all the world. All Christians belong to it, whether they have a denominational label or not. If they have been born of the Spirit of God they are members of the church, and there is only one church. Therefore, wherever the members meet one another, they already belong to each other. Whether you have your name on a church roll somewhere is of no significance whatsoever.

The second thing to strike you as you look at your own body is that it has members. It isn't just a trunk, but it has arms, legs, feet, toes, fingers, eyes, ears, and a number of other interesting protuberances. And they are all for a purpose. They are part of the body; they belong to the body. So also, the church of Christ has many members, and they are different from one another. This is what I like about the church—the diversity of its members. Yet this idea is so contrary to the spirit of the age, which is one of conformity. Everyone is pressured to look, act, talk, and think alike. Join a club and you have to dress as they dress, drive the same kind of car, and so on. Join another club and you have to change your way of speaking. I don't know why we have this mentality forcing us to duplicate everything. Even in the church people want to turn out Christians like so many sausages—all alike.

But this is not God's idea of the church. His idea is to have diversity within the church: many members, and none of them alike. That's the joy of it. They don't come from the same class or the same race; they are not the same color, and they don't even have the same gifts. They have many gifts. We are to recognize this diversity and rejoice in it.

And yet, Paul says, though these members do not all have the same function, each one belongs to all the others. No other organization in the world can say that about itself. In all other organizations, people become members for what they can get out of it. But in the church of Jesus Christ, we belong to one another. We share with one another. Paul says we are to have the same care one for another. Isn't this remarkable! How terrible it would be if all Christians were exactly the same.

Years ago our high school pastor was teaching 1 Corinthians 12 to some of the kids. To illustrate his point he painted a football like a huge human eye, with a big round pupil. He wrapped it in a blanket and put it under his arm and showed it to the kids. "What do you think of my baby?" he asked. They would look inside the blanket and see this huge eye staring out at them, and say "Oh, gross!" He also asked them, "What if your girlfriend was just an eye? When you took her out to eat, this great big eye would be sitting across from you in the booth. What a date that would be!" He drove home his point: We are not just one member; we are many. All the body is not an eye. Yet we are to have the same care one for another. Even though we are different, we are to love each other because we belong to each other. We share the same life.

This is why we are to get along with other Christians—not because we like them necessarily, or because they are nice, but just because we belong to each other. They are your brothers and sisters. When they hurt, you will hurt—whether you know it or not. And when they are honored you will be honored—whether you know it or not.

A number of years ago I fell and severely injured my wrist. It swelled up and became very painful. The rest of my body felt so bad about it that it sat up all night to keep my wrist company. This is what the body of Christ is to do when one member is hurt. We are tied to one another, and when one hurts, all hurt.

Graceful Functions

Paul goes on to point out what determines our function within the body:

> *We have different gifts, according to the grace given us. If a man's gift is prophesying, let him use it in proportion to his faith. If it is serving, let him serve; if it is teaching, let him teach; if it is encouraging, let him encourage; if it is contributing to the needs of others, let him give generously; if it is leadership, let him govern diligently; if it is showing mercy, let him do it cheerfully (12:6-8).*

This is only a sampling of gifts. Many others are mentioned in 1 Corinthians 12, 1 Peter 4, and Ephesians 4. You must put them together to get the total list of available gifts. But the point the apostle makes is this: God has given the gifts, and we have different gifts according to the specific grace given to each of us.

Paul literally calls these gifts *graces,* and I like this term because of what it says. Graces are graceful. Something graceful is a delight to watch, and this is true about a spiritual gift. A gift is an ability God has given because he wants you to function along that line. It enables you to do something so naturally, smoothly, and beautifully that others will take note of it and ask you to do it and enjoy watching you do it. And you will enjoy doing it. When you use your spiritual gift you are fulfilled. It is called a "grace" because it is not a difficult, painful thing to do; it is something you delight in doing. And you can improve in it as you do it. Therefore it makes life interesting and fulfilling.

Imagine how hurt you would be if you prepared gifts for your children, wrapped them all up in beautiful packages and put them under the Christmas tree, handed them out to your children on Christmas morning—and they immediately laid the packages aside and never bothered to open them. Can you imagine how the Lord must feel, having given us gifts to use, when we never take the trouble to find out what they are and never put them to work, excusing ourselves by saying we can't do anything? The Word of God tells us that not a single Christian is left out in this distribution of gifts. It is clear from this account that the gifts Paul lists are intended to be used.

The first gift mentioned is prophesying. In 1 Corinthians 12 and 14 Paul tells us this is one of the best gifts of all. This is the gift you ought to desire earnestly to have exercised in your midst, because it is the gift of expounding Scripture, making Scripture come alive. It comes from a word in Greek meaning "to say" and derives from a root meaning "to cause to shine." It refers to the ability to take the Word of God and make it shine. Thus everyone sees what to do and where to go and how to act and function. Peter says, "we have a more sure word of prophecy that shines as a light in a dark place." John Calvin describes prophecy as "the peculiar gift of explaining revelation." Paul says if you have the gift, use it. It is not just for people who go to seminary; others in a congregation may also have the gift of prophesying. Then use it. But you must use it according to the proportion of your faith. Stay with what you know. Don't try to get into areas you don't yet understand. That will come later as you grow in the use of your gift. Start where you do understand Scripture, make it clear to people, explain it. This is the gift of prophesying.

Some have the gift of serving. This is a beautiful and common gift. Many people have it. I believe it is the same gift called "the gift of helps" in 1 Corinthians 12. It is the word from which we get our word "deacon." It is "to deaconize," to serve as an usher, to do banking on behalf of the church, to care for widows, or to serve on committees. Serving is the ability to help people with such a cheerful spirit that they are blessed by it. All of us know people like this. We love to have them around because they are so eager to serve and they do it so willingly and cheerfully that everyone is helped and blessed by them. What a tremendous gift!

Find an Occasion

"If [his gift] is teaching, let him teach." Teaching is the ability to impart knowledge and information, to instruct the mind. Prophesying goes much deeper. It instructs the heart and moves the will. But teaching instructs the mind and is the basis for understanding many of the truths of Scriptures. Therefore the gift of teaching is a great gift, and widely distributed in the body. I suspect at least thirty percent or more of all Christians have the gift of teaching. If you have it, don't wait for someone to ask you to teach. The church didn't give you these gifts. God gave them to you—your responsibility is to put them to work. Don't wait for someone to invite you to exercise your gift. This may happen (and be glad if it does!), but you still have the responsibility to use the gift God has given you, whether anyone asks you to or not. *You* find the occasion. Find someone who doesn't know as much as you know and teach him, if you have the gift of teaching.

The gift Barnabas had was the gift of encouragement. He was called "the son of encouragement,"

which is what Barnabas means. His real name was
Joseph, but no one called him Joe; they called him
Barney. In the Scriptures he is always found with his
arm around someone's shoulder, encouraging him,
comforting him, urging him on. This is a marvelous
gift in the church. If you have the gift of encouragement, start anywhere and use it. God gave it to you,
therefore use it.

Another gift is that of giving, contributing. Did
you know this was a gift? It means God will give you
something to give as well as a desire to give it. If you
have this gift, use it! The more you use it, the more
you'll have to give. It is part of the way you function
in the body of Christ, and many can benefit from it.
Paul says, "Let him give generously," or according to
the literal meaning, "Let him give with simplicity."
It means without ostentation, without calling
people's attention to it. I heard of a man who stood
up in a meeting and said, "I want to give a hundred
dollars—anonymously." Someone with the gift of
giving can't give this way. If you have the gift of giving you are to give with simplicity, without making
a big deal out of it. Just give the gift as unto God and
delight in the opportunity to be used by the hand of
God.

Then the gift of leadership is mentioned. Specifically, this word means "leading meetings." It comes
from a root which means "to stand up before others."
If you have this gift, all kinds of meetings are waiting
for you to lead them. But when you use it, Paul says,
do it with diligence. Don't wing it. Do it thought-
fully; think it through in advance. Make yourself
ready for it and use the meeting to its fullest purpose.
The gift of leadership is a great gift.

Paul mentions finally the gift of showing mercy. I
delight in some of the people in our church who have

this gift. A young girl comes and brings retarded children, sits with them in her lap, and interprets the service to them. Another young girl almost every Sunday brings a dear old lady who is partially crippled and nearly blind. Mercy, you see, is helping the undeserving and neglected. The gift of showing mercy is a marvelous gift within the church, and many have it. If you have it, don't wait for someone to show you what to do—start doing it.

Sometimes great and marvelous organizations have grown up out of a single person beginning to exercise his gift. A ministry for physically and men-tally handicapped children, called *Green Pastures,* has grown up out of our church by the exercise of the gift of mercy by a single individual. Another ministry is reaching out to the vast crowd of homosexuals in our area. It was organized by someone who had a vision, a gift of showing mercy—someone who had an un-derstanding of the homosexual's need and a desire to help. These people are starting out alone, but others will join them.

Speaking or Serving

Many other gifts are not mentioned here. But no matter where you find a list of gifts, it is always divided into two parts. Peter mentions this division in 1 Peter 4:10-11. He says, "Each one should use whatever spiritual gift he has received to serve others, faithfully administering God's grace in its various forms. If anyone speaks, he should do it as one speak-ing the very words of God. If anyone serves, he should do it with the strength God provides, so that in all things God may be praised through Jesus Christ." These two divisions are *speaking* and *serving.* In Romans 12 the first four gifts listed have to do with speaking; the last three have to do with serving.

These, then, are the two basic functions of the believers in the body of Christ. Either you speak, or you serve—one or the other. And everyone is to be involved. Dr. F. B. Meyer, a great Bible teacher of the last generation, said this about the local church:

> *It is urgently needful that the Christian people of our charge should come to understand that they are not a company of invalids, to be wheeled about, or fed by hand, cosseted, nursed, and comforted, the minister being the Head Physician and Nurse; but a garrison in an enemy's country, every soul of which should have some post of duty, at which he should be prepared to make any sacrifice rather than quitting.*

This is a biblical picture of the church, a church functioning as God intended it to function.

Now we come to this question: Who are you, anyway? Every morning you ought to ask yourself that. Who am I? Your answer should come from the Scriptures: "I am a son of God among the sons of men. I am equipped with the power of God to labor today. In the very work given to me today God will be with me, doing it through me. I am gifted with special abilities to help people in various areas, and I don't have to wait until Sunday to use these gifts. I can use them anywhere. I can exercise the gift God has given me as soon as I find out what it is, by taking note of my desires and by asking others what they see in me and by trying out various things. I am going to set myself to the lifelong task of keeping that gift busy."

Paul had to write to Timothy and say, "Stir up the gift within you that was given you by the Holy Spirit." Perhaps Timothy was letting it slide. But we are expected to stir it up. I hope you present your bodies afresh today, so you can find that gift and put it to work. Be busy doing what God has sent you here to do. Perhaps you want to renew your request to God to help you in the search for your spiritual gift and to lead you to put it to work, recalling the day when you stand before him and he asks, "What did you do with the gift I gave you?"

9
HOW TO HUG

(Romans 12:9-21)

The title of this chapter, "How to Hug," was suggested by a story I once heard. A man walking down a street passed a used book store, and saw a book in the window with this title, *How to Hug.* Being somewhat of a romantic, he went in to buy the book. To his chagrin, he discovered it was a certain volume of an encyclopedia covering subjects beginning with the words "How" through "Hug."

I have often thought of the church like this. Everyone knows the church is a place where love ought to be shown. Many people have come to church hoping to find a demonstration of love, only to discover an encyclopedia on theology. But I am grateful God is changing the situation today. Thank God, hugs are returning to the churches. In the early church Christians actually greeted one another with a holy kiss. You don't see that too often these days, but perhaps it is coming back.

Love without Wax

The theme of Romans 12:9-21 is clearly given in the very first sentence: "Love must be sincere." Our English word "sincere" comes from the Latin *sincerus*—without wax. The word literally reflects what the Greek says here, "Let love be without hypocrisy." The Revised Standard Version translates it, "Let love be genuine." Phillips says, "Let us have no imitation Christian love."

In character, the early Christian community was primarily a place where love was demonstrated—so much so that people began to imitate it. Every writer in the New Testament stresses the need for love. In 1 Timothy 1:5, Paul writes to his young son in the faith and says, "The end of our endeavor is love." This is where it all comes out. "The end of our endeavor is love, out of a pure heart, a good conscience and a sincere faith." Peter says, "Above all, love each other deeply" (1 Peter 4:8). Paul reminds us here and in other places that this love must be genuine, not phony nor hypocritical.

In those early days of the church it was easy to imitate love if you didn't really have it. People fell into the habit, as they do today, of pretending love, using loving terms and gestures, but really not feeling it in their hearts. This, of course, is hypocrisy, and this is what this passage in Romans warns against. Don't let your love be hypocritical, don't put it on.

Hypocrisy—the false projecting of an image—is the spirit of our times. Through the mass media we are actually encouraged to be something we are not. No one seems to care how phony this is. But in the church it is intolerable. To be in any sense phony in our love is a violation of all the Lord came to do. Sham love, of course, comes from the flesh, that pretender down inside all of us that wants to be thought well of even though we are not really worthy of it. So we easily succumb to this desire.

But true love comes from the Holy Spirit. In Romans 5, Paul says, "The love of God is shed abroad in our hearts by the Holy Spirit which is given unto us." True love comes by learning from the word of God how you should behave in a certain situation, and then depending on the Spirit of God to give you the strength to move out and do this very thing. This is the way you love—by acting in obedience to what the Scriptures tell you by the power of the Holy Spirit within you.

This is what we are exhorted to do in this passage. Verses 9 through 13 set forth love in the family of God, the church. Verses 14 through 21 describe how Christian love looks when it is out in the world. First, love in the church is described:

> *Love must be sincere. Hate what is evil; cling to what is good. Be devoted to one another in brotherly love. Honor one another above yourselves. Never be lacking in zeal, but keep your spiritual fervor, serving the Lord. Be joyful in hope, patient in affliction, faithful in prayer. Share with God's people who are in need. Practice hospitality (12:9-13).*

Notice all that is involved in genuine love. First, true love rejects sin, but not the person who sins. This is what Paul means when he says, "Hate what is evil; cling to what is good." He is talking about people. That is, hate what is evil in people, but don't reject the person because of the evil. The person is good. God loves him. He or she is made in the image of God. Therefore, true love learns to hate evil but not to reject the good. I grant you this is difficult. But hypocritical love, love pretending to be Christian, does the opposite.

Hypocritical love is never extended to a person unless he behaves according to an acceptable standard. This is one of the things in churches that has turned people off more than anything else. People come and hear the great words of the New Testament about love and peace and joy and expect to find them exhibited, but instead they find all the world's attitudes—rejection, prejudice, and even contempt. Christians cut them off and set them aside, not wanting to have anything to do with them because they don't meet a certain standard of performance. This is what we are warned against. It is hypocrisy to reject persons because you don't like their behavior.

But you can go the other extreme in this as well. It is hypocritical to condone sin because you accept the person. Christians often realize it is wrong to cut people off and have nothing to do with them because they are not behaving properly, so some Christians accept these people and say nothing about their evil or sin, and even defend it. We see something of this today concerning homosexuality and alcoholism. People want to defend these sins, as though they were right, simply because they want to accept the person. "Hate what is evil [loathe it!]; but cling to what is good."

Second, true love remembers that *relationship* is the ground of concern, and not *friendship*. This is why Paul says, "Be devoted to one another in brotherly love." This does not refer to just anyone who is in need or in trouble; it specifies your brother or sister. The basis of concern for one another is not that we know each other well or enjoy one another; it is that we are related to one another, though we may never have met before. If we are Christians, we already have a tie that ought to evoke concern and care for one another.

Unlimited Good

Third, Paul says true love regards others as more deserving than yourself. "Honor one another above yourselves." Years ago I ran across a sign that has helped me many times. I have often been on the verge of pointing out that the credit for some idea belonged to me, but I have been stopped by remembering this little motto: "There is no limit to the good a man can do if he doesn't care who gets the credit." If you really don't care who gets the credit you can just enjoy yourself and do all kinds of good. Just be glad it is done, and don't worry about who gets the credit. Again, our flesh doesn't like this; it is very eager to be acknowledged and promoted. But God's Word tells us real love will not act that way.

Fourth, real love retains enthusiasm despite setbacks. "Never be lacking in zeal, but keep your spiritual fervor, serving the Lord." One of the most noticeable marks of a Christian walking in the Spirit is that he retains enthusiasm, always rejoicing in hope. He never lets his spiritual zeal flag or sag. The one thing the Lord cannot put up with, as he tells us in the letters to the churches in Revelation, is lukewarmness. It is nauseating. He will spew you out of his mouth if you are indifferent, neither hot nor cold, just going along with the crowd. Jesus says lukewarmness angers him.

I have always enjoyed the Old Testament story of

David and Goliath. Remember how all Israel was
sunk in despair through fear of this giant? The whole
army was helpless because of this man's taunts. But
young David was fearless. He was not afraid. He
looked at Goliath, in all his impressive height and
great strength, and asked, "Who is this uncircum-
cised Philistine, who dares defy the armies of the living God? Who does he think he is?" Now where did
David get this kind of enthusiastic response? David
tells us when he says, "The battle is not ours but the
Lord's."

This is what Paul is saying here. It is not your
battle; it is the Lord's. His resources, not yours, are
required to work it out. After all, why should you be
afraid or distressed or want to give up? It doesn't depend on you. You are serving the Lord! This is why it
is important to note what Paul is saying here. He reminds us of this fact: the only way to keep our enthusiasm high is to be aware we are serving the Lord.

Fifth, true love rejoices in hope. "Be joyful in
hope, patient in affliction, faithful in prayer." The
way to rejoice in hope is explained by the two other
things mentioned here. When trials come, begin
with prayer. As Paul tells us in Philippians, "In
everything, by prayer and supplication with
thanksgiving, make your requests known unto God"
(Philippians 4:6 RSV). Take them to him. If you are
faithful in prayer, you can be patient in affliction.
You won't be dropping out, or copping out, or quitting, but you will hang in there, waiting until God
works it out, not getting impatient, angry, or resent-
ful, but quietly waiting for God to accomplish what
he had in mind. This, of course, will make you rejoice in hope—because you will discover God has a
thousand and one different ways of working things
out, ways you can never imagine. This makes you re-

joice. You rejoice because God knows what he is doing and he is able to work it out.

Sixth, true love responds to needs. "Share with God's people who are in need. Practice hospitality." In these days when we have so much social help available—unemployment insurance, Social Security, welfare, Medicare, and so on—we tend to forget there are still unmet human needs that we have a responsibility to meet. We need to be reminded at times that people are still hurting and that it is a Christian's direct responsibility to care for their needs.

These are the ways to show love in the church. Let me review them quickly for you: (1) True love rejects sin but not persons; (2) it remembers that relationship is the ground of concern; (3) it regards others as more deserving than oneself; (4) it retains enthusiasm despite setbacks; (5) it rejoices in hope by being patient in affliction and faithful in prayer; and (6) it responds to needs in direct and personal ways, and especially by practicing hospitality.

Now Paul moves on to describe love amid a non-Christian world. Again, he gives us six ways to do this:

> *Bless those who persecute you; bless and do not curse. Rejoice with those who rejoice; mourn with those who mourn. Live in harmony with one another. Do not be proud, but be willing to associate with people of low position. Do not be conceited.*

> *Do not repay anyone evil for evil. Be careful to do what is right in the eyes of everybody. If it is possible, as far as it depends on you, live at peace with everyone. Do not take revenge, my friends, but leave room for God's wrath, for it is written:*

*"It is mine to avenge, I will repay," says the
Lord. On the contrary:*

*"If your enemy is hungry, feed him;
    if he is thirsty, give him something
        to drink.
In doing this, you will heap burning coals
    on his head."*

*Do not be overcome by evil, but overcome evil with
good (12:14-21).*

First, love speaks well of its persecutors. This is a
tough one, isn't it? "Bless those who persecute you;
bless and do not curse." This gets right down to
where the rubber meets the road! It means you do not
go around badmouthing people who are not nice to
you. You don't run them down or speak harshly
about them to others, but you speak well of them.
You find something you can approve, and you say so
to others.

I confess this is not my natural reaction. When
someone persecutes me, I want to persecute back!
But God's Word tells us we don't need to do this and
should not do this. It applies even to such practical
areas as traffic problems. Have you ever been persecuted in traffic? It happens all the time. Someone cuts
you off, and you want to roll down the window and
shout, "Melonhead!" But according to this passage,
you are not supposed to react this way. Now the passage doesn't tell you what to call him, but it does tell
you to bless him. Not sarcastically, but in reality.

Rejoicing Is Harder

Second, true love adjusts to others' moods. "Rejoice with those who rejoice; mourn with those who
mourn." When someone in your office is feeling low

and gloomy, don't come in and sit down and whistle away. When they obviously don't respond, don't ask, "What's the matter with you? How come you're so down all the time? Why don't you be cheerful like me?" When something has gone wrong, nothing is worst to have around than a cheerful person. No, Paul says, adjust yourself. Mourn with those who mourn, and rejoice with those who rejoice. I think he puts rejoicing first because it is so hard to do sometimes—especially if it awakens our envy or self-pity. If someone else has achieved something we think we ought to have, it is hard to go up to that person and say, "I'm so glad for you." But this is what love does, and it is possible to do it—for those who walk in the Spirit.

Third, true love does not show partiality. Paul says very precisely, "Live in harmony with one another. Don't be proud, but be willing to associate with people of low position. Don't be conceited." When Jesus came to Jerusalem he stayed with Mary and Martha and Lazarus out in the little suburb of Bethany instead of at the Intercontinental Hotel in Jerusalem. This is the attitude the apostle enjoins Christians to have. And he suggests that the real reason for respecting persons and for namedropping is really personal conceit. "Don't be conceited," he says. "Don't think highly of yourself." This is what makes you always want to be associated with the upper echelons of society. But if you have an honest view of yourself, you know you are no better than anyone else and therefore you will be willing to enjoy ordinary people. And you will find a rich love and humanity among them.

Fourth, love is not sneaky or underhanded (12:17). Paul tells us not to give back evil for evil, but to plan to do right, out in the open, before all.

"Do not repay anyone evil for evil. Be careful to do what is right in the eyes of everybody." Here Paul tells us not to take silent revenge for imagined or real insults and not to resort to subterfuges to get even.

Fifth, true love seeks to live at peace with everyone. "If it is possible, as far as it depends on you, live at peace with everyone." Some people just will not allow you to be at peace with them—but don't let it start with you. Remember the old song, "It Takes Two to Tango"? I think that last word ought to be "tangle." It takes two to tangle. If you refuse to tangle, at least the conflict will not arise with you and won't be traceable to your actions and your attitudes. This is what love really does.

Escalated Conflict

Last, love does not try to get even. Listen to these words again: "Do not take revenge, my friends, but leave room for God's wrath, for it is written, 'It is mine to avenge, I will repay,' says the Lord." Revenge is one of the most natural of human responses to hurt or injury or bad attitudes. We always feel that if we treat others according to the way they have treated us, we are only treating them as they deserve. We can justify this so easily. "I'm only teaching them a lesson. I'm only showing them how I feel. I'm only giving back what they've given me."

But any time you argue this way you have forgotten the many times you have injured others without getting caught yourself. But God hasn't forgotten. This always puts us in the place of those Pharisees who, when the woman was taken in adultery, were ready to stone her to death. Jesus said to them, "He that is without sin among you, let him cast the first stone." This stopped them all dead in their tracks, because all of them were equally guilty. They needed to be judged too. We must never carry out revenge, because we are not in the position of a judge. Since we too are guilty, we need to be judged. Therefore, Paul's admonition is, "Don't try to avenge yourself." You will only make a mess of it. The inevitable result of trying to get even is that you escalate the conflict. It is inescapable.

As a boy in Montana I used to watch the cows in the corral. They would stand peacefully until one cow would kick another cow. Of course, that cow had to kick back. Then the first cow kicked harder and missed the second cow and hit a third. That cow kicked back. I watched this happen many times. One single cow kicking another soon had the whole corral kicking and milling and mooing, all mad as could be. This happens in congregations too.

Paul gives two reasons why you should not avenge yourself. One is because God is already doing it. "Leave room for God's wrath." God knows you have been insulted or hurt or injured. He knows it and he is already doing something about it. Second, God alone claims the right to vengeance because he alone can work it without unnecessary injury to all concerned. Since he will do it in a redemptive way, he won't injure the other person, but will bring good out of it. Too often we fail to give God a chance; we take the matter into our own hands. Paul says such an action is wrong because we don't want that person to be redeemed; we want him to be hurt. We are like Jonah when Ninevah repented. When God spared the city, Jonah became angry with God. "Why didn't you wipe them out like you said you would?" Paul reminds us that God is already avenging, so we should leave him room. God claims the right to vengeance because he alone can work it without injury to all concerned.

You ask, "What do you expect me to do? Somebody hits me—do you expect me just to sit there and do nothing?" Oh no, there is something you should do. Look what it is: "On the contrary: 'If your enemy is hungry, feed him; if he is thirsty, give him something to drink. In doing this, you will heap burning coals on his head.' Do not be overcome by evil, but overcome evil with good" (12:20-21).

To Make Him Ashamed

Two things will happen if you refuse to avenge yourself and instead let God do it. First, you will be enabled to act positively instead of negatively. This will result in what Paul, quoting Proverbs 25:21-22, calls "heaping burning coals on his head." This does not mean you are going to get even by another process—burning his head. This refers to the ancient way of lighting fires. They did not have matches in those days, so if you wanted to light a fire in your home you couldn't go and simply borrow a match. But you could go and borrow some coals from your neighbor. Of course, you took along an earthen jar that would not burn. Then you would ask your neighbor if you could borrow some coals to light your own fire. If he was a good neighbor, he would fill the jar and you would carry the padded jar home on top of your head. This became a picture of an ample, generous response to a neighbor's need. Soon it became a metaphor for responding so generously to your neighbor that it made him ashamed of himself of his attitude toward you. This is what Paul is suggesting here.

The second result of leaving vengeance to God is that you win the battle. You will win a conflict if you respond by doing good instead of evil. One day I read a story about a Christian soldier who as a boy had

formed the habit of praying beside his bed before he
went to sleep. He kept up this practice in the army,
but he became an object of mockery and ridicule to
the entire barracks. One night he knelt to pray after a
long, weary march. As he was praying, one of his tor-
mentors took off his muddy boots and threw them at
the boy, one at a time, hitting him on each side of his
head. Saying nothing about it, the Christian lad took
the boots and put them beside his bed and continued
to pray. But the next morning, when the other man
woke up, he found his boots sitting beside his bed,
all shined and polished. It so melted his heart that he
came to the boy and asked him for forgiveness. This
led, after a time, to the man becoming a Christian.
This is what Paul means when he says you are to overcome evil with good.

Three times in this passage—in verses 14, 17 and
21—the apostle has stressed that we are not to return
evil for evil. So throughout this passage it is under-
scored that the major way we express love in the
world is by not reacting in vengeance when we are
mistreated by the world. Can you imagine what
would happen if Christians would begin to act this
way? Surely this is a practical way Paul has of reminding us not to be conformed to this age. We are not to
think like others do. When Jesus was reviled, "he reviled not again, but committed himself to him who
judges righteously" (1 Peter 2:23 KJV). This record
was given for our admonition, that we might behave
as Jesus did in the midst of the world. What a testimony of grace that would be!

10
GOD'S STRANGE SERVANTS

(Romans 13:1-7)

Our study of Romans has brought us to the famous passage in chapter 13 dealing with Christians and their relationship to the government. It is not hard to think of Senator Mark Hatfield of Oregon as a servant of God. His personal profession of a new birth has been well publicized. But have you ever thought of Mikhail Gorbachev as a servant of God? Or Idi Amin? Or even Adolf Hitler? And yet, amazingly, this passage declares that men like these are, in some sense, servants of God.

The first thing the apostle tells us about government is its source. Where does it originate? The answer is given in the very first verse:

*Everyone must submit himself to the governing
authorities, for there is no authority except that
which God has established. The authorities that
exist have been established by God.*

When Paul refers to "governing authorities" he
uses a phrase best translated as "the powers that be."
He is not simply talking about heads of state, but
about all levels of authority, all the way down to the
local dog catcher. These are the powers that be, the
powers that exist. We must realize that these governmental offices are in some way brought into being
by God himself.

No Best Form

We Americans love to think democracy is the most
God-honored form of government. But you can't establish that from Scripture. In fact, the Scriptures
support various forms of government. So which is the
best? A monarchy? An oligarchy (rule by a few)? A
republic? A democracy? Scripture's answer is not
necessarily any of these. The best form of government
for a nation is whatever God has brought into being.
This is best for that nation's particular place and time
in history. God has brought it into being, considering the makeup of the people, the degree of truth and
light disseminated among them, and the prevailing
moral conditions.

Not every body of people in the world is best
served by democracy. There was a time when Americans naively thought democracy was the best and
only enlightened form of government, and all we had
to do was go around the world and set up democracies
and people would begin to function properly.
Democracy would solve all their problems. Now,
after many painful experiences, we know better. For

some people in certain times and places, democracy just will not work, and God in his wisdom does not give it to them. The government they have is better suited for them than ours would be.

Of course, God can change the government. He does not ordain any one form of government to continue forever. If the people grow in understanding truth, and morality prevails in a community, the form of government may well take on a more democratic character. But when truth disappears, government seems to become more autocratic. In any case, the apostle makes the point that whatever form of government you find, God is behind it. Therefore we need to see that no government is in itself opposed to God. That includes communism as well as any other form of government.

This truth is not confined to the New Testament. Just before Daniel was to go before King Nebuchadnezzar—one of the most autocratic of kings—he prayed to God and said, "Blessed be the name of God for ever and ever . . . He changes times and seasons; he removes kings and sets up kings" (Daniel 2:20-21 RSV). Daniel's words make it clear that God determines who a nation's leaders will be. Sometimes we are tempted (or even taught) to think of God as being remote from political affairs, but Scripture never takes this position. God is not on some distant Mount Olympus; he is right among us, directly involved in the changing patterns of governments, raising up some and putting down others.

Paul wrote this letter to Christians living in the empire's capital city, Rome itself. By this time the Roman world had already passed through several forms of government. It had been a monarchy, a republic, and a principality, and now it was an empire.

Nero had just begun his reign as Rome's fifth emperor. Paul is telling the Christians of this time to remember that God is behind whatever form of government is in control.

Bad Men Too

God is behind not only the form of government, but also the very people who occupy the government offices. This may be a startling thought for some of us, but it is what this verse says. The New English Bible translates the last half of verse 1, "There is no authority but by act of God, and the existing authorities are instituted by him." These people in authority are put there by God.

So if you thank God for godly leaders like Mark Hatfield, remember that he also gave us Richard Nixon, Spiro Agnew, and all the others who have disappointed our trust. They, too, came from God. The biblical picture is that God by his grace not only sends us good leaders at times, but also bad leaders at other times to punish us. And we deserve them. When ruthless tyrants like Hitler and Stalin come to power, God has put them there because they are what people need at this time in history.

This is the startling biblical position. It is the clear statement of this passage as well as others. Peter says we are to "honor the king" (1 Peter 2:17), and Peter also was writing while Nero was seated on the throne. Christians are to be subject to the governing authorities, Peter tells us.

In Daniel we are taught the same thing. In a great decree issued by King Nebuchadnezzar throughout his kingdom, he testified how he had been brought low before God, and that God had taught him painful lessons until he learned "that the Most High rules the kingdom of men, and gives it to whom he will"

(Daniel 4:17 RSV). So the first thing we need to recognize is that regardless of the form of government we may be up against, the hand of God is in it. And this is true not only of the form of government, but also of the very ones who occupy its positions of power. God has put them there.

The second thing we need to know about our relationship to government is found in verse 2:

> *Consequently, he who rebels against the authority is rebelling against what God has instituted, and those who do so will bring judgment on themselves.*

If God is behind governments, then those who oppose the government to overthrow it are really opposing God. I realize this must be handled very carefully, because some would use such a statement to justify everything the government does, no matter what. But first we must recognize that governments have a God-given right to punish treason, to control riots, and to seek to preserve themselves in power by legitimate means. Governments have this right.

Punishment within Limits

Although Paul does not go into it here, we must also remember Scripture's teaching that such a right is always held under God. I thank God for the enlightened soul who, a few decades ago, began the movement to add the words "under God" to our pledge of allegiance. This reflects biblical truth. It is only under God that we exist as a nation. This means those who rule are to recognize they have limited power. They are agents of God, but they are not God.

There are some things nations have no right to do. The Bible makes it clear what these are. This is what Jesus referred to in the famous incident when he was asked about paying taxes. He held up a coin and asked, "Whose image is on the coin?" His audience said, "Caesar's." He said, "All right, then give to Caesar the things that belong to Caesar; but give to God the things that belong to God." By this he taught that government power is limited. Caesar has his image on certain things; therefore they belong to him—and rightfully so. What Caesar put his image on belongs to Caesar. But God has put his image on men; they belong to him. So men may give certain things to Caesar, but the men themselves belong to God and should rightfully give themselves to him.

Governments have authority over what we do with our property and how we behave with one another, but our Lord says they have no right to touch what God has put his image on: the spirit of man. In other words, Caesar has no right to require men to worship him, or to forbid their obedience to the Word of God. Rulers are under God; therefore they have no right to command men to do what God says ought not to be done. These are the limits of governmental power. Governments are not to enslave men, because men belong to God. Governments are not to oppress men, because men bear the image of God. What bears God's image must be given to God, and not to Caesar—just as what bears Caesar's image must be given to Caesar, and not necessarily to God. Though Paul in Romans 13 doesn't deal at length with this, he teaches that believers have a right to resist oppression and religious persecution by nonviolent means as they have opportunity. But we are not to resist the legitimate functions of government. We are to accept government as a gift of God.

The legitimate functions of government are further described in verse 3:

> *For rulers hold no terror for those who do right,*
> *but for those who do wrong. Do you want to be*
> *free from fear of the one in authority? Then do*
> *what is right and he will commend you.*

Do you hear what Paul is saying? If you are driving
down the freeway and want to be free from having to
look constantly in your rearview mirror, then keep
down your speed! The officer will pull you aside and
say, "Sir, you were driving so beautifully I just want
to commend you." Well, no, he won't do that. He
may wish he had time to, but he will just pass by and
wave at you. Verse 4 says:

> *For he is God's servant to do you good. But if you*
> *do wrong, be afraid, for he does not bear the*
> *sword for nothing. He is God's servant, an agent*
> *of wrath to bring punishment on the wrongdoer.*

To Preserve Security

In this very helpful passage, we learn that government has two basic functions. First, governments are
to protect us from evil, preserving our security. They
are to guard us against attack from without and crime
from within. For this purpose, governments properly
have armies and police systems and courts of justice.

In verse 6 we see a second function of government:

> *This is also why you pay taxes, for the authorities*
> *are God's servants, who give their full time to*
> *governing.*

Notice that Paul has three times called government agents "the servants of God." In verses 3 and 4,
he used the Greek word from which we get our word
"deacon." They are the deacons of God. The next
time you are called up in traffic court, view the judge
as a deacon of God. He is a servant.

The point these verses make is that these authorities exist as an arm of God's work. This not only involves punishment of crime and wrongdoing, but also commendation. Governments are to honor those who live as good citizens.

Even courts often recognize the right motives of people. I once read about a man on trial for stealing a loaf of bread. The man had no job, his family was hungry, he had tried to get work but couldn't, and tried to get funds for relief but couldn't, so he had stolen the bread to feed his family. When the judge learned of the circumstances, he said, "I'm sorry, but the law can make no exceptions. You stole, and therefore I have to punish you. I assess a fine of ten dollars. But I want to pay the money myself." He reached into his pocket, pulled out a ten-dollar bill, and handed it to the man. As soon as the man took the money, the judge said, "Now, I also want to remit the fine." The man could keep the money. "Furthermore, I am going to instruct the bailiff to pass a hat to everyone in this courtroom; I am fining everybody fifty cents for living in a city where a man has to steal in order to have bread to eat." When the money was collected, he gave it to the defendant.

That represents the good side of justice, a court that will on occasion recognize people's right motives even in doing wrong. This is a legitimate function of government. The government also has the right "to insure domestic tranquility" and "provide for the common defense," as the Constitution phrases it.

To Serve as Priests

A second basic function of government is indicated in verse 6, in the word used for "servants." It is not the word "deacon" here; it is "minister." The government is to provide not only our defense and security, but also certain common services we all need—to function as ministers among us, helping us in our needs. Out of this grows the governmental functions of providing mail service, utilities, schools, relief agencies, and so on. These are all proper functions of government agencies.

By God's grace, governments have two powers which enable them to provide these services. First, they have authority to use force. This is what is meant by the phrase "he does not bear the sword for nothing." The sword is the symbol of the right to use force, even to the point of taking life. I think people are more confused about this right to use force than about any other government function. Take the question of capital punishment for example.

When the state, acting in line with the judicial system and functioning as it was intended to function, finally sentences an individual to yield his life for a certain crime, this is really not the same thing as a man taking another man's life. God is taking that life through the state. Let us remember God has the right to take human life. All through the Old Testament you find him doing this very thing. He also has the right to set up human channels for doing this. This means governments have the basic right to maintain armies for their defense, and that people— even Christians—are to serve in them.

Of course these powers can be (and have been) abused. Citizens have every right to protest these abuses and to seek to correct them. But it is folly to try to eliminate the rightful uses of authority simply because some of them are being abused. We should correct the abuses rather than eliminate what Scripture ordains.

The second power governments rightfully have from God is the power to collect taxes. You may not like the amount of taxes your government collects, but you can't object to the principle of taxation. Taxes are right, and governments have taxed their citizens from time immemorial, and will continue to do so. The apostle makes clear that the government has the right to collect taxes, and Christians should pay them.

Because of Conscience

The final Christian position respecting these things is summed up in verses 5 and 7. In verse 5 we see the attitude we are to have:

> *Therefore, it is necessary to submit to the authorities, not only because of possible punishment but also because of conscience.*

This has to do with our attitude about taxes, arrests, judicial systems, and so on. We are to obey the law not just because we are afraid of getting caught. We are to obey speed limits whether or not a police car is in sight. We are to pay our income taxes not merely because we know the government has tremendous computers that can review any number of records and can catch us if we don't. Because of this many more people are honest today about their taxes, but it ought not to be the Christian's reason for paying taxes honestly. The Christian's reason is that it is the right thing to do. Your conscience ought to be clear. You ought to pay the taxes because this is what God says to do, and not what man says.

Verse 7 tells us what actions should follow from this conviction:

> *Give everyone what you owe him: If you owe taxes, pay taxes; if revenue {that is, "hidden" taxes such as sales taxes, customs duties, and so*

*on}, then revenue; if respect, then respect; if
honor, then honor.*

Here the apostle deals with our response to these
demands of government. We haven't the right to
withhold taxes if the government doesn't use the
money quite the way we think it should. Governments are made up of fallible men and women just
like us, and we can't demand that the government always handle everything perfectly. So to these Romans, who had the same problems we have about
taxes, Paul writes, "If you owe taxes, pay them."

This point Paul makes about not resisting the
powers of government is set in the context of his word
in 12:2—"Be not conformed to this present age."
Don't act as everyone else acts about taxes. The world
grumbles and gripes and groans at paying taxes. You
have a right, of course, as does everyone, to protest
injustice and to correct abuse, but don't forever be
grumbling about the taxes you have to pay.

I have had to learn some lessons on this myself.
The first time I had to pay an income tax was many
years ago. My income had been so low for so long I
didn't have to pay any taxes. But gradually it caught
up and I finally had to pay. I remember how I re-
sented it. In fact, when I sent my tax form in I addressed it to "The Infernal Revenue Service." They
never answered, although they did accept the money.
The next year, I had improved my attitude a bit. I
addressed it to "The Eternal Revenue Service." But I
have repented from all those sins, and I now hope to
pay my taxes cheerfully.

I don't try to defend the gross injustices that pre-
vail in our American system. But the very fact we can
meet openly together to worship God and have relative freedom from attack wherever we walk about, is

due to the existence of a government God brought into being. As a good citizen I want to make every effort to improve it and see that it does things better. But I thank God for the privilege of paying taxes.

Someone has well said, "Every nation gets the government it deserves." So as we pay our taxes, let us do so cheerfully. And remember that the apostle tells us not only to pay our taxes, but also, if we owe respect, to give that; and if honor, to give that. Never forget that the worst governments are, nevertheless, better than anarchy, and serve certain functions which God himself has ordained. Therefore let us respond as Christians, with cheerfulness and gladness for what we can do under God, so people will see something different about us. Thus we commend ourselves to God and to all people.

11
THE NIGHT
IS NEARLY OVER

(Romans 13:8-14)

When Paul wrote this letter, surely love was the thing most lacking in the Roman Empire. These Roman Christians needed desperately to learn how to display love amid the pressures and oppression of their day. Love was needed also in the city of Corinth—the city from which Paul wrote the letter to the Romans—with its immoral sexual practices and its abandonment to pleasures. Today as well, the greatest need of men everywhere is to learn the secret of how to love. *Love makes a difference.*

Listen to what Paul says to these Romans in 13:8-10.

> *Let no debt remain outstanding, except the con-*
> *tinuing debt to love one another, for he who loves*
> *his fellow man has fulfilled the law. The com-*
> *mandments, "Do not commit adultery," "Do not*
> *murder," "Do not steal," "Do not covet," and*
> *whatever other commandment there may be, are*
> *summed up in this one rule: "Love your neighbor*
> *as yourself." Love does no harm to its neighbor.*
> *Therefore love is the fulfillment of the law.*

Have you ever struggled to obey the Ten Commandments? Have you found it difficult to face up to
obeying these commands not to murder or lie or steal
or commit adultery? Well, Paul says it is really easy.
All you have to do is love. Act in love toward people
and you won't hurt them. You can't. Love is the solution to all the problems we struggle with. Think of
what would happen in this world if people could be
taught how to love—and then did it?

The first result I can think of is that all the im-
pending divorces would soon be happily resolved.
Couples ready to split up because love has left their
marriage could go back together and learn how to
work it out. Think what would happen if all the di-
vorce problems pending in this country would suddenly be resolved and homes and families would be
secure!

If we could teach people how to love we would no
longer fight wars. We wouldn't have to worry about
disarmament. We could send the atom bombs and
nuclear explosives and missiles off into space somewhere and let them join the rest of the space garbage.
What a remarkable thing this would be! Think of
how much energy and money is being expended in
keeping up this endless array of armaments simply
because we can't trust people to love each other.

If we could love each other, crime would disappear. The streets would be safe for pedestrians once more, and in all the great cities of our land we would feel safe and secure. All the money we spend on prisons and reformatories could be be spent on something more useful. And we wouldn't need any courts of law or police—except to regulate traffic now and then.

And think what would happen to our tax burden if we could get rid of all wars and crimes and police and courts! Taxes would be reduced to practically nothing! All the money poured into taxes today could be used to spread beauty and harmony of life to everyone on earth. Our biggest problem is our lack of love, our inability to love one another.

This passage tells us that the ability to love—and nothing less—is the radical force Jesus Christ has turned loose in this world by his resurrection. It has the power to radically change the world. Paul implies that this change must start with us. If we are Christians, if we know Jesus Christ, we have the power to love. You need never doubt this. If you know him, you have the power to love. You don't have to ask for it; you've got it. If you have Christ, you have the ability to act in love, even when you are tempted not to.

The Debt You Owe

Therefore, Paul says, when you rub shoulders with people, remember that your first obligation is to love them. Act in love. Show courtesy, kindness, patience, understanding, longsuffering—whatever it takes, whatever the scene demands, you can show it. It is a debt you owe that person. "Owe no man anything but to love one another." We are to think of this as our obligation to everyone. I wonder what radical things would start happening among us if we were to start living on this basis, if we would say to ourselves every day, every time we meet someone, "I need to show love to this person. No matter what else happens, I have an obligation to pay him this debt."

I have noticed that whenever I am together with people I owe money to the first thing coming to my mind is the debt I owe them, and I wonder if this is what they are thinking about too! Paul says we are to think about love in this way. We are to remember we have an obligation to love.

The second thing Paul says is that this obligation is to everyone. This is intended for your neighbor. Who is your neighbor? You think immediately of the people who live on each side of you. They are your neighbors, because they live next door to you. They are in contact with you. But many others are in contact with you as well. The people sitting next to you in church are your neighbors, for the moment at least, and so are the people you meet in business, and in your shopping. Wherever you are, the people you meet are your neighbors. The word to us is that since we have the ability to love, we are to love our neighbor as ourselves. The butcher, the baker, the Cadillac maker—it makes no difference, they are all your neighbors.

Beyond the Law

The third thing Paul says is that when you love like this you fulfill the law and even go beyond the law. The law says to you, "Don't injure your neighbor." You can do what you like with your own property, but it stops at your neighbor's line. You can't do what you like with his. If you do, you are answerable to the law. But love goes a step beyond. It doesn't stop with the negative, "Don't injure your neighbor"; it says, "Do good to your neighbor." Love him, reach out to him, minister to him, help him. It is simply impossible to love your neighbor and harm him at the same time.

Thus, love will not sleep with your neighbor's wife or husband. Love will not murder your neighbor, or poison his dog, or throw garbage over the fence into his back yard, or do anything harmful to him. Love will not steal from your neighbor, or keep his lawn mower for more than a month. Love will not covet what is your neighbor's; it won't drool over his pool, or stew about his new Porsche. Love does not want what your neighbor has, but rejoices with him over what he has. Love, therefore, fulfills the law. You don't have to worry about keeping the Ten Commandments; all you have to worry about is acting in love, paying the debt you owe every man, every woman, every child, every person you meet. If you pay the debt of love you will not injure them.

Furthermore, Paul says:

> *And do this, understanding the present time. The hour has come for you to wake up from your slumber, because our salvation is nearer now than when we first believed. The night is nearly over; the day is almost here. So let us put aside the deeds of darkness and put on the armor of light. Let us behave decently, as in the daytime, not in orgies and drunkenness, not in sexual immorality and debauchery, not in dissension and jealousy. Rather, clothe yourselves with the Lord Jesus Christ, and do not think about how to gratify the desires of the sinful nature (13:11-14).*

What strikes me most in this passage is the opening sentence. Love your neighbor, Paul says, and pay the debt you owe him, *understanding the present time.* Something about the age we live in, if you understand it, will compel you, motivate you, drive you to love your neighbor. If you understand the times, you will be helped to do this.

Paul points out three things about the times. First, he says it is time to get going: "The hour has come for you to wake up from your slumber, because our salvation is nearer now than when we first believed. The night is nearly over; the day is almost here."

It is time to wake up, time to get going, time to look around and recognize all the opportunities to love. I am amazed to see how many times in my own life I pass over an opportunity to love. I am always looking for opportunities with other people out there, further away. Yet I am surrounded in my own family with opportunities to show love, even when it is difficult. Christians are called to love the unlovely—those who for the moment are not themselves acting in love. How easy it is for people to want to help someone farther away and ignore the needs right around them. A couple brought some clothes down to our church one day to take to the Rescue Mission. The lady was very concerned about the poor people's need for proper clothing, but I noticed her husband had to hold up his pants with a nail!

Now, we don't have much time to do this reaching out. The time is short. As Paul puts it, "Our salvation is nearer than when we first believed." The deliverance we look for when Christ returns is nearer than when we first believed. The Christian message has been going out for nearly two thousand years—and now how much nearer we are to the time when Christ is coming back! "The night is nearly over," Paul says, "The day is almost here." On one occasion Jesus said, "I must work the works of my Father while it is day. The night is coming, when no man can work." Jesus was aware of the urgency of his labor, because the day was almost gone.

On another occasion he said, "As long as I am in the world, I am the light of the world." When Jesus was present on earth, it was daytime. But when he left us physically, when he was buried in the grave, the night came. The night has been running on now for more than nineteen hundred years. As the apostle Paul tells us in his letter to the Colossians, Christians are to be like lights shining in the darkness of the night. The night is all around us, but the day is about to come. The night is nearly over; the day is at hand.

The Edge of Eternity

You say, "Wait a minute. Paul wrote this letter nineteen hundred years ago, and he said it was nearly over then. How could it have been nearly over when nineteen hundred years have gone by?" From that point of view, it is hard to understand. But in a sense these words are always true of every one of us. I am sure this is the way the apostle meant them for himself. Regardless of whether Jesus Christ returns in this generation to fulfill his promise, the truth is that the night is nearly over for each of us. When our brief life ends the day dawns.

For those of us who have a few gray hairs, the night is nearly over; the day is at hand. If we are ever going to love, it has to be now. We can't wait much longer. But how about young people, fresh and strong and filled with excitement and energy? I often think of the words of George Bernard Shaw: "Youth is such a wonderful thing, it's a shame to waste it on the young." But how much time do young people have? Who knows? We all live on the edge of eternity. The night may be nearly over for any one of us, no matter whether we are old or young. So the argument of the apostle is powerful. He is saying, "If you are going to love, now is the time to do it. You can't wait for to-morrow. Start now to love one another. The night is nearly over; the day is at hand."

The second thing we need to understand is that now is the time to abandon some things.

> *So let us put aside the deeds of darkness and put on the armor of light. Let us behave decently, as in the daytime, not in orgies and drunkenness, not in sexual immorality and debauchery, not in dissension and jealousy (13:12-13).*

If you are going to live in love, certain things must go: things that are incompatible with love. You can't do them and love at the same time. Paul suggests three categories:

First, "Don't live for empty and harmful pleasures. Give up orgies and drunkenness." That covers a whole spectrum of things, and means: "Don't devote your life to seeking good times, things you plan over and over again for your own self-indulgence, an end-less round of parties or plays or concerts, or even watching television." You can't love and do that. Such a course is wasting your life. You have only so many precious moments to show this mighty power, this release, this radical power of love. If you spend your moments in endless self-indulgence you will never be able to live in love.

Too Easily Pleased

Second, "Don't live for sex." Sex is a powerful force that is highly exploited today. We are constantly sur-rounded with silken and sensuous temptations—a new affair, a new romance, a new liaison to satisfy us, please us, fulfill us. The world urges us to try it; they tell us there is no harm in it. But Paul says there is. He says if you live for them, you can't fulfill what God wants you to fulfill. You will miss the excitement and the radical glory of loving people. You can't love people and live for sex. Paul covers the whole range of immorality here—fornication, adultery, homosexuality, pornography. If you indulge in them, you cannot love; you will destroy others and destroy yourself. To experience the glory of what God wants you to have, it is essential to lay aside these cheapening, tawdry things. C. S. Lewis well says,

> *We are half-hearted creatures, fooling around with drink and sex and ambition, when infinite joy is offered us. Like an ignorant child who wants to go on making mud pies in a slum because he cannot imagine what is meant by the offer of a holiday at the sea, we are far too easily pleased.*

The *third* category is this: "Don't live for strife, dissension and jealousy." It amazes me how many people, including Christians, get their kicks out of being the cause of dissension. They can't seem to enjoy themselves unless they get people fighting and upset and angry—either with them or with one another. A word from Jesus has always helped me when I am tempted along these lines: "He that is with me gathers; but he that is against me scatters." What is your effect upon people? Do you harmonize them? Do you gather them together? Are they noticeably happier because you have come in? Or do strife, division, and separation immediately break out when you are there? What is your life doing? This is how you can tell whether you are with Jesus or against him. If you are with him, you gather people; if you are against him, you scatter them.

Paul says it is time not only to get going and to give up, but also, above all else, time to *put on*:

Rather, clothe yourselves with the Lord Jesus Christ, and do not think about how to gratify the desires of the sinful nature (13:14).

When I get up in the morning I put on my clothes, intending them to be part of me all day, to go where I go and do what I do. They cover me and make me presentable to others. That is the purpose of clothes. In the same way, the apostle says to us, "Put on Jesus Christ when you get up in the morning. Make him a part of your life today, going with you everywhere you go and acting through you in everything you do. Call upon his resources. Live your life *in Christ*." This is the way to love.

Notice that Paul uses the full name, "the Lord Jesus Christ." I think he does this deliberately. "Lord" stands for Christ's power to rule, his authority, his power to change and alter events, to control history, "to open, and no man shuts; to shut, and no man opens." When you put on the Lord you are putting on power you would not have without him, power to change events and affect people.

When you put on "Jesus" you are putting on the capacity to love. Jesus would put his hand on a loathsome leper to heal him, even though the law forbade it. Jesus would reach out to the lost woman and the drunkard and speak a healing word in their lives. He treated the lowly the same as he did the higher-ups. Jesus loved people. People everywhere were struck with his compassion. When you put on Jesus, you are putting on the capacity to love.

When you put on "Christ" you are putting on the power to deliver. Christ means "Messiah," or "anointed." It refers to his work: Christ came to deliver us, to set us free. When you put on Christ, you have an amazing power to free yourself and others from despair in the midst of difficult circumstances.

So put on the Lord Jesus Christ. Remind yourself of his presence all through the day. Reckon on his power to supply love when you begin to obey the command to love. And, as Paul says, "Do not think about how to gratify the desires of the sinful nature." Stop planning for evil and self-indulgence, for it always ends in strife and rivalry, jealousy and debauchery. Rather, learn to love by putting on the Lord Jesus Christ.

"Take and Read"

"Take and read"—these words have been made famous by their connection with the fourth-century conversion of Saint Augustine. Augustine as a young man was what we would call a playboy. He lived a wild, carousing life, running around with evil companions, doing everything they were doing. He denied himself nothing. And just as such people do today, he came to hate himself for it.

One day he was pacing up and down in a garden, bemoaning his inability to change: "O, tomorrow, tomorrow, tomorrow! How can I free myself from these terrible urges within me that drive me to the things that hurt me!" In his despair, he suddenly heard what he thought was the voice of a child—perhaps some children were playing in the garden next door—and the voice said, "Take and read, take and read." He could not remember any children's games with words like that, but the words stuck. Turning back to a table in the garden, he found lying there a copy of Paul's letter to the Romans. Flipping it open, he read these words:

> *Let us behave decently, as in the daytime, not in
> orgies and drunkenness, not in sexual immorality
> and debauchery, not in dissension and jealousy.
> Rather, clothe yourselves with the Lord Jesus
> Christ (13:13-14).*

Augustine said that at this moment he opened his
life to Christ. He had known about him, but had
never surrendered to him till this moment, and when
he did, he felt a healing touch from Christ cleansing
his life. He was never the same again.

This is what Jesus Christ is capable of doing. He
gives us power to love. If we but choose to exercise
this power in the moment of need, we release in the
world this radical force with power to change everything around us. It will change our homes, our lives,
our communities, our nations, the world—because a
risen Lord is available to us, to live through us.

J. B. Phillips translated this last verse beautifully:
"Let us be Christ's men from head to foot, and give
no chances to the flesh to have its fling."

This is the way to live!

12
ON TRYING TO CHANGE OTHERS

(Romans 14:1-12)

In Romans 14 Paul discusses the favorite indoor sport of Christians: trying to change each other! This problem has plagued the church throughout its history. It comes from thinking God is clearly pleased with the way we live—but others don't live like we do! They drink beer and play cards; they go to movies; they smoke cigars; they work on Sundays; they wear lipstick; they dance; they play musical instruments; they use zippers instead of buttons—the list has no end.

We are dealing, of course, with the problem of Christian taboos, the no-nos of the Christian life encountered from place to place and from time to time.

How much fellowship can you have with a Christian who lives in a different way than you do, who does things of which you do not approve?

The passage discussing these questions of Christian ethics is rather extensive—all of Romans 14 and the first fourteen verses of chapter 15—which in itself indicates the size of the problem. It is important to note that this whole section is part of an extended commentary by the apostle on Christ's command to love one another. This has been the subject ever since Paul turned to the practical part of this letter in Romans 12. There, you may remember, he tells us several things about love. First, the nature of love is to serve; we are given spiritual gifts so we might serve one another. Second, he tells us love must be genuine, not "put-on."

Then in Romans 13 we learn love must be submissive, especially to the powers that be, for they are put there by God. Later in the same chapter Paul tells us love must be universal; we owe love to everyone without exception.

Now in Romans 14 we learn that love must be patient and tolerant of other people's views. Think of someone whom you regard as less enlightened than yourself, then read what Paul says about them:

> *Accept him whose faith is weak, without passing judgment on disputable matters (14:1).*

This is plain, isn't it? Do not reject him; do not ignore him; do not treat him as a second-class citizen. Accept him, but not for the purpose of arguing with him. Accept him without passing judgment on disputable matters.

Accepting without Correcting

Regardless of how you may struggle with other Christians, you must realize they are brothers and sisters in the family of God. You did not make them part of the family—the Lord did. Therefore you are to accept them because they are your brothers and sisters, and not with the idea of immediately straightening them out. This is a necessary, practical admonition. Many of us love to argue and sometimes the first thing we want to do is straighten out the other person.

I remember a time years ago when I had finished preaching on a Sunday night, a man came up to me and said, "Let me ask you something. Do you believe two Christians who love the Lord and are led by the Holy Spirit will read a passage of Scripture and both come out believing the same thing?" I said, "Yes, I think that sounds logical." "Well," he said, "can you explain why I believe the passage you preached on tonight does not teach a millennium, when you believe it does? What do you think of that?"

Being young and aggressive I said, "Well, I think it means I believe the Bible and you do not." This immediately precipitated an argument, and with several other people gathered around we went at it hammer and tongs for an hour or so.

Afterward I realized how wrong I was. I had to write to this brother and tell him I was sorry I jumped on him like that. Of course he had jumped on me too, but that was his problem, not mine. I had to straighten out my problem, so I apologized to him and said, "I am sorry I did not recognize the parts where we agree before we got on to those things over which we differ."

Paul wants us to understand we are first of all to accept people, to let them know we see them as brothers or sisters. Acknowledge your relationship by some gesture or word of acceptance so they do not feel you are attacking them. The Greek here indicates we are not to accept people with an ulterior motive of arguing about our differences. The New English Bible phrases it, "without attempting to settle doubtful points." First, recognize the basic fact that you belong to one another.

Paul goes on in verse 2 to more precisely define the areas of debate he has in mind:

> *One man's faith allows him to eat everything, but another man, whose faith is weak, eats only vegetables.*

This is not dealing with nutrition, of course. In the early church whether to eat meat was a real moral question. They did not eat pork, and even beef and lamb had to be kosher—slain and processed in a certain way. So a Jew, or even a Christian reared as a Jew, always had great emotional difficulty in eating meat. I still wonder how Paul reacted when as a Christian he was first handed a ham sandwich!

In Rome and other pagan cities another problem was related to eating meat that had been offered to idols and later sold to the populace in butcher shops close to the temples. Some Christians said those who bought and ate this meat were no different from those who worshiped idols. But other Christians said, "How can that be? Meat is meat. Even if someone else thinks of it as offered to idols, I don't have to think of it that way."

The Broad and Narrow Views

In every such debate, it really does not make any difference what you are arguing about if the Scriptures themselves do not speak about it. You will always hear opposing views. Many of our modern problems can be put in this category. Should we drink wine and beer? Should we go to the movies? Should we dance? What about playing cards?

Let us be very clear that Scripture speaks about certain areas which are in no way debatable. It is always wrong to be drunk. It is always wrong to commit adultery or fornicate. In both the Old and New Testaments, God has spoken; he has judged these things. In these matters Christians are exhorted to rebuke and exhort and reprove one another—if necessary, even to discipline one another according to patterns set out in the Scriptures. This is not judging one another; the Word of God has judged, it has already pronounced what is wrong.

But other areas are left open. The wonderful thing to me is that Scripture always leaves them open. Paul will not give a "yes" or "no" about these things because God does not do so. In other words, God wants to leave certain matters to the individual. And he expects each person's decision to be based on deep personal conviction.

Paul regards the narrow party as being someone "weak in the faith." This has nothing to do with the strength or weakness of the individual's faith. Paul is talking about someone who is weak in *the* faith. This is a doctrinal problem; he does not understand truth.

Jesus himself said, "If you hold to my teaching, you are really my disciples. Then you will know the truth, and the truth will set you free" (John 8:31-32). The mark of understanding truth is freedom, and Paul says the person who understands truth is strong in the faith. Those who do not understand are weak in the faith. They do not understand the delivering character of truth.

William Barclay, in his commentary on Romans, has handled this well. He says:

> *Such a man is weak in the faith for two reasons:*
> *(1) He has not yet discovered the meaning of*
> *Christian freedom; he is at heart still a legalist;*

> *he sees Christianity as a thing of rules and regulations. His whole aim is to govern his life by a series of laws and observances; he is indeed frightened of Christian freedom and Christian liberty. (2) He has not yet liberated himself from a belief in the efficacy of works. In his heart he believes that he can gain God's favor by doing certain things and abstaining from others. Basically, he is still trying to earn a right relationship with God, and has not yet accepted the way of grace. He is still thinking of what he can do for God more than of what God has done for him.*

The contrast here is between a Christian who has not yet understood the freedom Christ has brought him, who feels limited in his ability to use certain things, and the man who recognizes his God-given freedom. One is strong in the faith; the other is weak in the faith. Every church has these groups, and Paul puts his finger precisely on the natural attitudes we must avoid if we are going to accept one another. In verse 3 he says,

> *The man who eats everything must not look down on him who does not.*

The first thing is that the strong must not reject the one who is still struggling, who is still weak. The word translated "look down on" here really means "to push out." The strong must not push him out; he must not exclude him. The strong must not think about him in a disdainful or contemptuous way.

Not Deliberate Weaklings

Some of us who feel free in certain of these areas tend to regard those who are not yet free as weaklings, which in some sense they are. But we are not to treat them as if it is their own fault they are that way.

It is wrong to become offended when they do not behave as freely as we think they should. Paul says, "The strong must not reject the weak."

Someone has defined a legalist as a person who lives in mortal terror that someone, somewhere, is enjoying himself. But we must not think of legalists this way, because this is not their motivation. We are not to exclude these people in our contacts. We must not form little cliques within the church, or think of our group as being set free while this group over here is very narrow. Paul actually implies that if any of the so-called strong exclude weaker brothers, they have simply proved they are just as weak in the faith as the ones they have denied. Strength in the faith means more than understanding truth. It means acting in a loving way with those who are weak. The truly strong in the faith will never put down those who are still struggling.

On the other hand, the apostle states in verse 3,

> *The man who does not eat everything must not condemn the man who does, for God has accepted him.*

Here is the other side of it. Those who struggle must not look down on those who have freedom. Those who think it is morally wrong for a Christian to drink wine or beer must not look down on those who feel free to do so. They must not judge them. The word "condemn" means to sit in judgment, and it involves two things.

It involves, first, criticism or censuring. We are not to go up to people and say, "I do not see how you can be a Christian and do things like that." The word "condemn" also means categorizing people, classifying them as carnal Christians, reproving or rebuking them. In these areas we have no right to reprove or

rebuke. The church has no authority to impose be-
havioral standards or codes without the agreement of
all who might be affected by them.

Sometimes limitations have good reasons, but the
limitations must not be imposed on an individual by
other people. Often in a church those who are weak
in the faith, who do not fully understand their freedom in Christ, are the majority. They tend to make
artificial standards and impose them on everyone
else, implying that you cannot really be a Christian
unless you conform to these standards. This has happened widely in our day, and for the most part the
"narrow" party has triumphed in evangelical circles.

This has given rise to a tremendous distortion: The
world thinks Christianity is a "don't" religion. For
this reason many people won't touch the church with
a fifty-foot pole, though they are fantastically interested in the gospel.

Not My Brother's Judge

Now we come to the central part of this section.
The apostle explains three great facts, all supporting
and explaining the great principle of acceptance.

The first reason you must not look down on the
weak and judge or condemn the strong is that it is
not your responsibility to change your brother in this
area. He is not your servant. This is what Paul says in
verse 4:

> *Who are you to judge someone else's servant? To
> his own master he stands or falls. And he will
> stand, for the Lord is able to make him stand.*

The reason we are not to judge each other is that
we are not responsible for one another's conduct in
this area. Such responsibility is not defined in the
Scriptures. This is an open area that each one has to

decide for himself before God. The other person is not your servant, Paul says; the Lord chose him. The Lord, then, is responsible to change him. The Lord chose him without asking you or me.

But Paul's point (verse 4) is that the man under consideration is being changed. He is on his way to standing. "He will stand," Paul says. "Stand," of course, means he will be straightened out if he is doing wrong in any area. If it is really wrong, God will straighten him out. I enjoy the lapel pin Bill Gothard gives out with the letters P B P G I N F W M Y; that is, "Please be patient, God is not finished with me yet."

We are all in the process of change. The Lord is doing it and he will accomplish it. He is changing us, and if we will just wait a while we can see some of the changes. If the problem is a failure to understand truth, the solution is to teach the truth more plainly. As people hear it and understand it, they will be freed. To try to force them into reluctant compliance with something they do not yet understand is ridiculous and futile. Therefore be patient. If they are being exposed to truth, they will change. Let the Lord change them; it is his responsibility. Not only will he do so, but he is perfectly able to do so. Phillips once said: "God is well able to transform men into servants who are satisfactory."

Now if the first point is that it is not your responsibility to change these people, the second is that God reads the heart and he sees something you cannot see:

> One man considers one day more sacred than another; another man considers every day alike. Each one should be fully convinced in his own mind. He who regards one day as special, does so to the Lord. He who eats meat, eats to the Lord,

for he gives thanks to God; and he who abstains,
does so to the Lord, and gives thanks to God. For
none of us lives to himself alone and none of us
dies to himself alone. If we live, we live to the
Lord; and if we die, we die to the Lord. So,
whether we live or die, we belong to the Lord
(14:5-8).

This is an impressive point. God can read hearts
and you cannot. These distinctions and differences of
viewpoint arise out of honest convictions which God
sees even if you don't. The individual is not being
difficult simply because he does not agree with you.
He is acting on the basis of what he feels is right, so
give him the benefit of the doubt.

Believe that he is as intent on being real before
God and true to him as you are, and if he feels able to
do some of these things you think are not right, then
at least see him as doing so because he really believes
God is not displeased with him on that basis. Or, if
he does feel limited and thinks he should not do certain things, do not get upset with him because he has
not moved into your freedom yet. Remember that he
really feels God would be displeased if he did those
things; it is an honest conviction. The apostle makes
clear here that every man should have this kind of
conviction: "Let every man be fully persuaded in his
own heart."

This means you are not to act simply because you
were brought up a certain way or because you think it
right. Find some reason in Scripture for it. Seek justification out of the Word of God. You may change
your mind as your understanding of truth develops,
but at least let it be on the ground of a conviction of
the heart and mind.

Next Paul says that God sees both of these men and
both of these viewpoints as honoring him. The one

who thinks Sunday is a special day that ought to be kept distinct from all other days is doing so as unto the Lord. Therefore, honor and respect that viewpoint. On the other hand, someone may say, "No: when we are in Christ, days do not mean anything. They are not set aside for any special purpose. Therefore, I feel every day is alike, and I want to honor the Lord on every day." Do not be upset at this. He is expressing a deep conviction of his heart.

The one who drinks beer gives thanks to God for the refreshment of it and the taste of it, and this is perfectly proper. The one who says, "I cannot drink beer. I only drink coffee," gives thanks for the coffee. The coffee may do as much physical harm as the beer, but in either case it is not a moral question. It is a question of what the heart is doing in the eyes of God. Sometimes we are too harsh with one another in these areas.

Some time ago I heard of a converted nightclub singer, a fresh, new Christian, who was asked to sing at a church meeting. Wanting to do her very best for the Lord whom she had come to love, she dressed up the best way she knew how and sang a song that she thought expressed her faith. She did it in the "torchy" style of the nightclub singer. Someone came up to her afterward and ripped into her: "How can you sing a song like that and claim to be a Christian? God could never be happy with a Christian who dresses the way you do, and sings in a nightclub style." The poor girl stood for a minute, then broke into tears and turned and ran.

This was a wrong and hurtful thing to do to her. Later on, she might have changed her style, but God has the right to change her, and no one else. Her heart was right, and God saw her heart and honored it.

Liberty and Limitation

The last thing Paul says in this area is that our relationship with one another is more important than our lifestyle:

> *For none of us lives to himself alone and none of us dies to himself alone. If we live, we live to the Lord, and if we die, we die to the Lord. So, whether we live or die, we belong to the Lord (14:7-8).*

The apostle is saying here that living is liberty and dying is limitation. He is not talking about funerals and life and death in that sense. He is talking about those who feel free to enjoy liberty to the fullest. They are living, while others, because of deep convictions of their own, limit themselves, and thus are dying, because death is limitation.

"But whether we live," Paul says, "or whether we die, that is not the important thing. The important thing is that we belong to the Lord. He understands." Therefore, what we ought to remember in our relationships with one another is that we belong to the Lord. We are brothers and sisters; we are not servants of each other. Since we are servants of the Lord, he has the right to change us.

The third and final fact supporting this governing principle is that Christ alone has won the right to judge:

> *For this very reason, Christ died and returned to life so that he might be the Lord of both the dead and the living. You, then, why do you judge your brother? Or why do you look down on your brother? For we will all stand before God's judgment seat. It is written:*

> *"As surely as I live," says the Lord,*
> *"Every knee will bow before me;*
> *every tongue will confess to God."*
>
> *So then, each of us will give an account of himself*
> *to God (14:9-12).*

The Lord alone has the right to judge us in these areas. Because he has been involved in both death and life, he has the ability to do so. He died, so he knows what ultimate and utter limitation is. He gave himself up to death, and he deliberately restricted himself in many things, so he knows what death is like. And he lives, so he is free to do anything and everything he desires: he knows what life is like. Therefore, he alone has won the right to judge us. He alone understands us.

So Paul says, "Stop trying to take his place. Stop trying to be Christ to the rest of the church or playing God to each other. You, the weak, why do you judge your brother? And you, the strong, why do you look down on your brother? It is wrong. You are trying to take Christ's place when you do this. But remember that all of us, men and women alike, all brothers and sisters together, must individually stand before God's judgment seat."

This is true in both a present and future sense. We are before him all the time and we have to give an account to him and to him alone. But a day is also coming, as Paul mentions in 1 Corinthians 4, when "The Lord returns and brings to light all the hidden things of the heart." All the things we thought nobody ever saw will be brought to the light. We must then give an account to the Lord.

Again, Paul sums up everything in the first part: We are not servants of each other; we are brothers and sisters. We are all struggling, we are all in the process, we are all subject to change, we are all trying to understand truth more clearly as we go on, and we are all being freed by it. But in the process, the only one who has a right to do anything about it is the Lord. So we are to stop judging each other in these areas. Instead, we are to love one another and to show our love by accepting one another.

13
THE RIGHT
TO YIELD

(Romans 14:13-23)

Continuing the lengthy passage dealing with matters of individual conscience—dietary restrictions, certain rituals, and so forth—Paul discusses what we can do about these matters. How are we to behave toward one another in these areas? The first thing we can do is given in 14:13.

> *Therefore let us stop passing judgment on one another. Instead, make up your mind not to put any stumbling block or obstacle in your brother's way.*

I have always appreciated that Scripture is never merely negative. It never says "Do not do something" without suggesting something positive to take its place. If all the apostle had to say was "Stop judging," it would be like telling someone "Do not worry" and nothing more. If you try to stop worrying without any reason for doing so, you will find yourself worrying all the more. Scripture does not merely say "Stop judging"; it says "Stop judging others; if you want to judge, start with yourself." Are you pushing liberty so hard, insisting on your rights and your freedom so much that you upset others and force them to act beyond their own conscience? What you ought to judge is the effect your attitude about some of these things has upon others.

The apostle goes on to give us two reasons why we must not judge others, but rather judge ourselves first. The first reason is in verse 14:

> *As one who is in the Lord Jesus, I am fully convinced that no food is unclean in itself. But if anyone regards something as unclean, then for him it is unclean.*

Here is a fundamental, psychological insight into life that ought to govern our behavior. It is one thing to be free yourself to partake of various things. You may have arrived at this freedom by some direct teaching of Scripture, even as Paul was taught by the Lord Jesus himself. What Paul really says is, "As one who has been taught by the Lord Jesus, no food is unclean in itself."

The Lord Jesus said, "No food is unclean." He did not mean any food is all right to eat—for some things you can eat are highly poisonous. Instead he meant the issue is not a moral one. Jesus himself taught this, and Paul says, "This is enough for me. It sets me free."

But that is not the only problem. The conscience needs to be trained by this new insight into liberty. One person's conscience may move much more slowly than another's; therefore, we are to adjust to one another's needs.

Crossing a Swinging Bridge

We can compare this to crossing a swinging bridge over a mountain stream. Some people can run across such a bridge even though it does not have handrails. They are not concerned about the swaying of the bridge, or the danger of falling into the torrent below. But others are very uncertain on such a bridge. They shake and tremble; they inch along. They may even get down on their hands and knees and crawl across. But they will make it if you just give them time, if you let them set their own speed. After a few crossings they begin to pick up courage, and eventually they are able to run right across.

It is the same way with these moral questions. Some people cannot see themselves acting in a certain area that they have been brought up to think is wrong. As in the case of the swinging bridge, it would be cruel for someone who had the freedom to cross boldly to take the arm of someone who was timid and force him to run across. He might even lose his balance and fall off the bridge. This is what Paul warns about in verse 15:

> *If your brother is distressed because of what you eat, you are no longer acting in love. Do not by your eating destroy your brother for whom Christ died.*

It is wrong to do that. It is not loving to force people to move at your pace. To refuse for someone else's sake to indulge in a freedom—to adjust to his pace—is surely one of the clearest and truest exercises of Christian love.

Divisions over Minor Matters

The second thing Paul says is that the issue of freedom versus nonfreedom does not demand unyielding firmness:

> *Do not allow what you consider good to be spoken of as evil. For the kingdom of God is not a matter of eating and drinking, but of righteousness, peace and joy in the Holy Spirit, because anyone who serves Christ in this way is pleasing to God and approved by men (14:16-18).*

If you are going to create division by arguing so hard for your rights and your freedom, or by flaunting your liberty in the face of those who do not agree with it, then you are distorting the gospel itself, Paul argues. He actually uses the word "blaspheme." You are causing what is good—the good news about Christ—to be blasphemed because you are making an issue over a minor matter. You are making your rights so important that you have to divide the church over them, or separate from a brother or sister who does not believe as you do. In so doing you are saying to the watching world that Christianity consists of whether you do or do not do a certain thing.

I once heard of a church that got into an unholy argument over whether to have a Christmas tree at their Christmas program. Some thought a tree was fine; others thought it was pagan. They became so angry at each other they actually had fistfights over it. One group dragged the tree out, then the other group dragged it back in. They ended up suing each other in a court of law and, of course, the whole thing was in the newspaper for the entire community to read. What else could non-Christians conclude but that the gospel consists of whether or not you have a Christmas tree?

Paul says this is utterly wrong. The main point of the Christian faith is not eating or drinking or having Christmas trees. The main point is righteousness and peace and joy in the Holy Spirit. A non-Christian, looking at a Christian, ought to see these things; not wrangling and disputing and fighting and law courts, but righteousness.

You have seen this word *righteousness* many times in Romans, and you know it means God's gift to you of worth. Because of the death of Jesus on your behalf you are loved by him; you are accepted by him; you are a valuable person in his sight. In fact, he cheerfully and delightedly calls you his beloved child. This is righteousness, and from it comes a sense of dignity and self-respect. The world ought to see you confident, with a kind of underlying assurance that is without conceit. It will show you have a basis of self-acceptance the world knows nothing about.

The second thing the world ought to see is peace. This comes visibly as a kind of calmness, an inner core of unflappability that is undisturbed by the minor irritations of the moment. It comes from a quiet assurance that God is present in the situation; that he will work it out for his glory, and therefore, we need not get upset, angry, or vindictive. It is hard for the world to get this impression of peace and calmness if they see two people screaming at one another over some issue.

God-given Delight

The third element is joy. These three always go together: righteousness, peace, and joy; they are gifts of God. They do not come from you, but from him.

Joy is the delight in God that always finds life worthwhile though it may be filled with problems.

Joy in a Christian does not come from circumstances. I will never forget meeting a lady who had been lying in her bed for thirteen years. Her arthritis was so bad her joints were disconnected, and she could not even raise her hands. But the smile on her face was an outstanding witness that joy of this kind is a gift of God. It comes out of relationship, not out of circumstance. Because of this joy she had a tremendous ministry to the community around her.

Paul is saying that if you have that relationship as the center of your focus and interest, you can easily give up some momentary indulgence that might bother someone or make him move beyond his own conscience. Paul's words here should be to us mentally like the traffic sign that says YIELD. This is what we are to do. The Christian philosophy is to yield, to give way. Do not insist on your rights.

In the second section, verses 19-21, Paul gives us guidelines to follow. Two guidelines are listed in verse 19:

> *Let us therefore make every effort to do what leads to peace and to mutual edification.*

The first guideline is in the phrase "what leads to peace." Enjoy your liberties, indulge them wherever you desire, if you can do so without destroying someone else's peace. Enlarging on this idea, Paul goes on to say,

> *Do not destroy the work of God for the sake of food.*

Peace is the work of God. Nothing can produce lasting peace among people, especially those of different cultural backgrounds, except the work of God.

It is the Spirit of God who produces peace. If you destroy this peace for the sake of some right of yours, some liberty you feel, you are destroying what God has brought about. Do not do that; it is not worth the struggle.

The apostle's second guideline is to stop exercising your liberty whenever it arrests someone else's learning process. All Christians ought to examine these issues more and more. They ought to investigate for new truth from God's Word, constantly keeping an open mind. And they will, if we do not push them too hard. But if someone flaunts his liberty in such a way as to anger people and upset them, it will often harden their resistance to change so they no longer want to examine the question. Paul says this must be the limit to those who exercise their liberty. Do not push people that far, or press them that hard. Rather, we are to help them understand the reason for our liberty.

Healthy Indulgence

I think it is healthy for a Christian who has liberty in some of these areas to indulge it on occasion. The cause of Christ is never advanced by having every strong Christian in a congregation completely forego his right to enjoy some of these things. What happens then is that the question is settled on the basis of the most narrow and most prejudiced person in the congregation. Soon the gospel itself becomes identified with that view. So the outside world often considers Christians narrow-minded people with no concern except to prevent enjoyment of the good gifts God has given us.

It is a good thing for people to indulge their liberties. Such action raises questions in the minds of those who are not free, especially when they see this indulgence linked with a clear demonstration of righteousness and peace and joy in the Holy Spirit. It makes them think when they see a godly person whom they admire and respect indulging freely in something they have never been able to indulge in. Yet they cannot deny he is godly. It is good for them to be forced to rethink their prejudices.

But Paul says to be careful, and judge how far you are going. If what you are doing upsets people and hardens them in their views so they will no longer examine and investigate, then stop—you are going too far. That should be the limit. This is what the apostle means when he says, "all food is clean, but it is wrong for a man to eat anything that causes someone else to stumble. It is better not to eat meat or drink wine or do anything else that will cause your brother to fall."

Notice Paul does not say it is wrong to make him *think*; it is never wrong to indulge your liberty to such a degree that your brother questions his viewpoint. But it is wrong to persist to such a degree you cause him to act beyond his convictions. That is causing him to fall.

Paul brings in the third guideline in verses 22 and 23:

> *So whatever you believe about these things keep between yourself and God.*

This translation suggests you are to keep quiet about your liberties; but what Paul is saying is that if you have faith, have it between yourself and God. That is, let God and God's Word be the basis for your faith, and nothing else. Be sure what you are doing is not because of pride, because you want to show off how free you are. You are doing this because God has freed you by his Word. Paul says,

> *Blessed is the man who does not condemn himself*
> *by what he approves.*

If you have really based your action on God's Word, then your conscience will be free. You will not feel guilty and troubled as to whether you are acting beyond what the Word of God really says. You will be happy, free, blessed.

"But," Pauls says,

> *the man who has doubts is condemned if he eats,*
> *because his eating is not from faith; and every-*
> *thing that does not come from faith is sin*
> *(14:23).*

If you have not really settled this on the basis of Scripture, but are acting only because you want to indulge yourself, or if you like this thing but you still feel a bit troubled by it—you will be condemned by your conscience. And if you are condemned by your conscience, you will feel guilty. And if you act even though you feel guilty, you are not acting out of faith; therefore, you are sinning. This is Paul's argument.

"Without faith," Hebrews says, "it is impossible to please God" (Hebrews 11:6). Faith means believing what God has said. You must base your actions in Christian liberty on what the Word of God declares—not about any specific thing, but upon the great principle of freedom which is set forth there.

To sum up, what Paul has said to us is this: First, do not deliberately shock your brothers or sisters. Do not deliberately do things to offend them, or even make them feel uncomfortable. Think about them, not yourself.

Second: Give up your right when it threatens the peace or hinders the growth of another. Be alert to judge in this area.

Third: Never act from doubt. Act only from conviction, by the Scriptures and by the Spirit of God. If all these problems are settled on this basis, a congregation will move gradually toward the great liberty we have as children of God.

What will happen in the eyes of the watching world? Christians will be seen as free people, not controlled by regulations that limit and narrow them in their enjoyment of God's great gifts. Nor will these things be so important that they are put at the heart of everything. The world will begin to see the gospel is righteousness and peace and joy in the Holy Spirit, the gifts of God. These gifts, then, are the basis for freedom in all these areas.

You are just as free to say No to the indulgence of a liberty as you are to say Yes to it. This is true freedom. You are not free if you think you must have your rights. That is not freedom. Freedom is the ability to give up your rights, for good and proper cause. This is what the watching world will see.

14
OUR GREAT EXAMPLE

(Romans 15:1-13)

The fifteenth chapter of Romans concludes Paul's discussion on how to decide what is wrong and what is right for Christians. He summarizes his argument thus far in the first two verses of the chapter:

We who are strong ought to bear with the failings of the weak and not to please ourselves. Each of us should please his neighbor for his good, to build him up.

When you have to make a quick decision whether to insist on liberty in a certain area or give way to someone else's qualms, two thumbnail rules will help. The first rule is: Choose to please your neighbor rather than yourself. After all, this is what love does. Love does not insist on its own rights, Paul tells us in 1 Corinthians 13. If you are loving in your approach, you will adjust and adapt to others. J. B. Phillips' translation of this verse puts it well:

> *We who have strong faith ought to shoulder the burden of the doubts and qualms of the weak, and not just to go our own sweet way.*

The second rule, however, says to be careful that your giving in does not allow your neighbor to entrench his weakness. Do not leave him without encouragement to grow, or to rethink his position. Please your neighbor, but for his own good. Always leave something to challenge his thinking or make him reach out a bit. His viewpoint just may change.

On a recent visit to Sacramento I talked with a teacher in a Christian school. He had been asked by the school board to enforce a rule prohibiting students from wearing their hair long. He did not agree with the rule, and found himself in a serious dilemma. If he did not enforce the rule the board told him he would lose his job. If he did enforce it he would upset the students and their parents. Though our culture has long since changed from regarding long hair as a symbol of rebellion, this man found himself between a rock and a hard place. His plea to me was, "What shall I do?"

My counsel was that he should not push his idea of liberty to the point that it upset the peace. I said to him, "For the sake of peace, go along with the school board and enforce the rule for this year. But make a strong plea to the board to rethink their position and to change their viewpoint. At the end of the year, if they are unwilling to do that, perhaps you might well consider moving to a different place, or getting another position. That way you would not upset things or create a division or a faction within the school."

Example from the Past

These decisions are not easy to make, but we can find ways to work out these problems. To encourage us, Paul gives three factors we can count on for help. The first is the example from the past:

> For even Christ did not please himself but, as it is written: "The insults of those who insult you have fallen on me." For everything that was written in the past was written to teach us, so that through endurance and the encouragement of the Scriptures we might have hope (15:3-4).

The first example is Jesus himself. Even though he was perfect, Jesus ran into this kind of problem. Even though he never on any occasion displeased God the Father to the slightest degree, nevertheless he encountered plenty of antagonism. As Paul says, Jesus fulfilled the Scriptures which predicted that those who did not like God's methods would take it out on him. "The insults of those who insult you," he says, "have fallen on me." Thus, our Lord had to bear with the unhappiness and even the insults of those who could not be pleased even with what God himself was doing.

In Luke 14, for example, the Pharisees accused Jesus of not keeping the Sabbath properly. They were upset because he did things they thought were inappropriate for the Sabbath. What did our Lord do? Did he give in to their desire? No, he ignored their protest and did things that upset them even more. If he had gone along with them they would never have learned what God intended the Sabbath to be. So the Lord did not always adjust to their antagonism.

But on another occasion the Lord was accused of not paying his taxes. When the disciples told him about this he sent Peter down to the lake to catch a fish, and in the fish's mouth he would find a coin sufficient to pay the tax for both Peter and himself. Jesus said he did this in order not to offend them. That is, he adjusted to their custom at this point. If we think we have difficulty in applying these rules, we must remember the Lord himself had difficulty.

On still a third occasion he publicly acknowledged there was no way to please everyone: Jesus said, "When John the Baptist came to you, he came neither eating nor drinking." This does not mean John did not eat food but that he carefully observed certain dietary restrictions. He was probably a Nazarite who had taken a vow never to touch any alcoholic beverage. So Jesus said, "When John came neither eating nor drinking, you said of him, 'He has a demon.' But when I came both eating and drinking, you called me a glutton and a drunkard. So how can I please you?" Jesus simply recognized the impossibility at times of adjusting to everyone. Thus he went ahead and did what God sent him to do, and let God take care of the difficulties.

Surely this is what Paul has in mind. He tells us our Lord is the example, and that at times you can't please anybody. At other times you can—and if you can, you should. But you should not seek to please other people if it would hinder them in their spiritual growth.

Yielding Graciously

Not only do we have our Lord's life as our example, but the Old Testament also helps us here, especially in yielding up our rights. Remember when Abraham and his nephew Lot stood looking over the valley of the Jordan River? It was necessary to divide the land between them. Abraham, who by right ought to have had the first choice, gave the choice to Lot. Lot chose the lush, beautiful, green areas of the Jordan valley, leaving Abraham the barren hills. So Abraham becomes an example of graciousness in that he gave up his rights.

Also Moses, according to the record, gave up his place as a prince in the household of Pharaoh. As Hebrews 11:25 tells us, he gave it up that he might "suffer reproach with the people of God for a season."

Remember David and Jonathan who were such close friends? We see Jonathan gracefully yielding his right to the throne to David, because he knew God had chosen him. Jonathan also supported him against the wrath of his own father. What a beautiful picture it is: Jonathan willing to give up so David might gain.

In a scene from the New Testament, John the Baptist says of Jesus, "He must increase; I must decrease" (John 3:30 KJV).

Yet none of these men ever really lost anything. By giving up, these men gained. They achieved God's objective, and God was glorified.

Not only do we get help from the past, but Paul goes on to show us the encouragement from the present as well:

> *May the God who gives endurance and encouragement give you a spirit of unity among yourselves as you follow Christ Jesus, so that with one heart and mouth you may glorify the God and Father of our Lord Jesus Christ (15:5-6).*

Paul says we need never panic, or fear we cannot work out these problems. God can drastically change the situation. He is that kind of God. The apostle suggests two things we can do when we get involved in a disagreement like this. First, pray for unity. Paul himself asks God to grant them "a spirit of unity among yourselves."

A Special Ministry of the Spirit

In Luke 11:13 Jesus said, "If you then, though you are evil, know how to give good gifts to your children, how much more will your Father in heaven give the Holy Spirit to those who ask him!" Jesus is talking here about times in your life when you need a special ministry from the Holy Spirit. "If you know how to give good gifts to your children, even though basically you have evil in your nature, how much more willing is the heavenly Father to give the Holy Spirit to you in times of problems and difficulties, to preserve the spirit of unity you desperately need."

Recently I learned of a serious difference of viewpoint between two brothers in Christ. Not only did it bring them to a deadlock, but it affected a whole program God was putting together, one that depended on their working together. It looked as though the whole thing would come to an ignoble end; nothing could be worked out. But others heard about this; and they and the two men involved began to pray, asking God to intervene. Then, at a final meeting scheduled to work this out, one of the men said, "There's no need for us to talk about this, because God has already been talking to me. He showed me I've been stubborn and obstinate about this, and I'm sorry. Let's go on to other things now; let's get the program started." The whole difficulty faded away because God is able to change situations and bring about unity. So prayer for unity is one of the most important things we can do in times of disagreement.

The second thing is to praise God for the relationship we already have, "so that with one heart and mouth you may glorify the God and Father of our Lord Jesus Christ." With one heart and mouth! Remember you are brothers. Thank God together for what unites you and minimize the things that divide you. Remember the important thing is to show a watching world the unity of brotherhood God has brought about. In Ephesians 4 we are admonished to be "eager to maintain the unity of the Spirit in the bond of peace." Encouragement in the present, then, comes from prayer, asking God for the spirit of unity, and praising him for the unity that already exists.

We have had encouragement from the past, and encouragement from the present, and now Paul tells us to be encouraged by what the future holds:

> *Accept one another, then, just as Christ accepted you, in order to bring praise to God. For I tell you that Christ has become a servant of the Jews on behalf of God's truth, to confirm the promises made to the patriarchs so that the Gentiles may glorify God for his mercy, as it is written:*
>
> > *"Therefore I will praise you among the Gentiles;*
> > *I will sing hymns to your name."*
>
> *Again, it says,*
>
> > *"Rejoice, O Gentiles, with his people."*
>
> *And again,*
>
> > *"Praise the Lord, all you Gentiles,*
> > *and sing praises to him, all you peoples."*

And again, Isaiah says,

*"The root of Jesse will spring up,
one who will arise to rule over the nations;
the Gentiles will hope in him"* (15:7-
12).

God is already working out a great program to re-
concile the Jews and the Gentiles. God has announced he is going to do it, and he will bring it to
pass. In fact, the program has already started. It
started when Christ accepted both Jews and Gentiles,
regardless of their great differences.

Separated by Hate

In Paul's day the Jews held the Gentiles in contempt; they called them dogs and would have nothing to do with them. The Jews even thought it a sin
to go into a Gentile's house, and they would never
dream of eating with a Gentile. They regarded Gentiles with utter contempt. The book of Acts tells us
how Peter got into serious trouble with his Jewish
friends because he went into the home of the centur-
ion Cornelius and ate with him. Peter was able to justify his conduct to his friends only because he could
show that the Holy Spirit had sent him there and
used him there.

Of course if the Jews felt this way about the Gentiles, the Gentiles paid it back in kind. They hated
the Jews. They called them names; this is where
modern anti-Semitism was born. Yet, Paul says, God
is healing this kind of division by the work of Jesus.

And how did Jesus do it? Paul's point is that Jesus
did his work by becoming a minister of the circumcision. The New International Version says he "became
a servant of the Jews." This is based on the idea that
what Paul wrote was, "Christ became a minister of

the circumcision," which is another name for the Jews. Actually what the text says is, "he became a minister of circumcision," which does not necessarily refer to the Jews as a people, but to their customs, rituals, and ceremonies, symbolized by the rite of circumcision.

The apostle argues that the Lord healed this breach between Jew and Gentile by giving in and limiting his own liberty. He who designed the human body, he who made it perfect, exactly as it ought to be, consented to the act of circumcision. His body was mutilated. That part of his body which was the sign of the flesh was cut off. Jesus consented to this limitation and became a circumcised Jew. Further, he who declared in his ministry that all foods are clean, and thus showed he understood the liberty God gives us in the matter of eating, never once ate anything but kosher food. He never had a ham sandwich for lunch or bacon for breakfast.

Even further, he who was without sin insisted on a sinner's baptism. John the Baptizer said to him, "Why are you coming to me? I need to be baptized by you. You do not need to be baptized." Jesus said, "Allow it to be so, for in this way it is fitting for us to fulfill all righteousness." So he who had no reason to be baptized nevertheless consented to be baptized.

Paul points out the results of this limitation: Jesus broke the back of the argument and contempt between the Jew and the Gentile. He reached both Jews and Gentiles to the glory of God. In the death and resurrection of Jesus, God showed his faithfulness to the Jews in fulfilling the promises made to the patriarchs. He also showed his mercy to the Gentiles, saving those who were without any promises at all. Thus the two, Jew and Gentile, shall fully become one, just as the Scriptures predict here. Paul gives quotations from the Psalms (the writings); from Deuteronomy (the Law); and from Isaiah (the prophets), all of which agree that God can work out these kinds of problems.

Then Paul concludes with this magnificent benediction:

> *May the God of hope fill you with all joy and peace as you trust in him, so that you may overflow with hope by the power of the Holy Spirit (15:13).*

What a magnificent verse! Whenever I am asked to give an autograph I almost always include this verse in it. Look how much you have going for you. All the great words of the Christian faith appear here: *hope* (twice, and the second time it is "overflowing" hope) and *joy* (all joy, great joy) and *peace* (calmness and confidence) and *trust* (belief in a living God) and finally, *the power of the Holy Spirit* (the invisible force that can open doors and no man shuts them, and can shut and no man opens—the power of God released among us).

I have been in places where the testimony of Christ in a community has been wrecked by the divisions and the attitudes of Christian people toward one another in these areas. When we presume to write one another off because someone has liberty we do not feel he should have; when we talk down to people and disparage those who do not have the faith and strength to act in liberty such as we do, we destroy the work of God.

The apostle urges us to unite on the great positive words of our faith. We are to allow these qualities of hope, joy, peace, trust, and power to be visible to others when we gather as Christians.

It might almost be said the letter to the Romans ends with this verse, Romans 15:13. It is true Paul goes on to give some personal words about his own ministry. But in a sense the whole argument of this epistle is drawn to a close with this tremendous benediction:

May the God of hope fill you with all joy and peace as you trust in him so that you may overflow with hope by the power of the Holy Spirit.

How I hope these words will characterize us to the world around!

15
AN ADEQUATE MINISTRY

(Romans 15:14-33)

We are drawing to the close of our study of this great epistle to the Romans. It closes just as it began, with a personal word from the apostle about himself and about the church in Rome. This closing section of chapter 15 has two themes: the church at Rome, and the ministry of the apostle Paul. Concerning the church, the apostle begins:

> *I myself am convinced, my brothers, that you yourselves are full of goodness, complete in knowledge and competent to instruct one another (15:14).*

You remember that the apostle began this letter by pointing out how the faith of these people was known around the world. Now in the fifteenth chapter, Paul gives us a further insight into this church. Here in verse 14 he says the church possessed three great qualities.

First: "I am convinced, my brothers, that you yourselves are full of goodness." Their motives were right. They had come to the place where they were motivated by goodness. This church at Rome was a responsive church, a compassionate church. It reached out to people in need, responding to those who had hurts and burdens.

No Theology Needed Here

The second thing the apostle says is that they were complete in knowledge. This is remarkable. Here was a church to which Paul did not need to give any new theology. Though Romans is one of the most deeply penetrating theological treatises in the New Testament, Paul did not write it because these people were doctrinally ignorant. They knew about the themes Paul emphasized in this letter, such as justification by faith—the gift of worth in God's sight. They knew it was not earned by trying to do good works before God—this is impossible, and they understood that. They knew they did not deserve anything from God, and yet they were his dearly loved children, and God accepted them fully.

They understood the nature of the flesh and the need for sanctification. Even though they had been redeemed, they knew they still possessed an old nature. The old Adam was still there, giving them trouble. Young Philip Melancthon, the colleague of Martin Luther, once wrote to Luther and said, "Old Adam is too strong for young Philip." These people at Rome understood this and they knew it would be a lifelong struggle. Paul did not have to tell them this; they knew it before he wrote.

They knew also God is working out a great plan, creating a wholly new humanity. Amidst the ruins of the old he was producing a new man, and they knew they were part of it. They understood the great themes of glorification, and of the eternal ages to come. So Paul writes and says they were complete in knowledge.

The third thing the apostle had to say about this church was that they were competent to instruct one another. He said, "You are able to counsel one another." This is the answer to the terrible pressure often placed upon pastors expected to solve all the problems of their congregations, and to counsel everyone firsthand. This was never God's intention. The plan of God is that the whole congregation be involved in the work of counseling. The whole congregation is to be aware of what is going on with neighbors and friends and brothers and sisters, and do something about meeting their problems through the use of their spiritual gifts. So the church at Rome had the right motives, they had complete knowledge, and they had the full range of gifts, so they were able to do many things within their church community and in the city of Rome.

But Paul also recognized three things they lacked:

> I have written you quite boldly on some points, as if to remind you of them again, because of the grace God gave me to be a minister of Christ Jesus to the Gentiles with the priestly duty of proclaiming the gospel of God, so that the Gentiles might become an offering acceptable to God, sanctified by the Holy Spirit (15:15-16).

You would think a church that was theologically knowledgeable, able to instruct and counsel one another in the deep problems of life, and filled with a spirit of goodness and compassion, would hardly need anything more said to them. Yet Paul wrote to such a church because they needed three other things.

Built-in Forgetfulness

First, they needed a bold reminder of the truth. "I have written you quite boldly on some points, to remind you of them again." I saw a man the other day, a grown man, with a string around his finger to remind him of something he wanted to be sure to remember. Forgetfulness is somehow built into our humanity. Surely one of the greatest proofs of the fall of man is that we have such a hard time remembering what we want to remember, yet so easily remember what we want to forget!

We need to be reminded again and again of the great themes of the gospel. Thus in Romans 12 Paul says, "You need your mind renewed by the Holy Spirit." This is one reason Christians gather in church meetings: We need to have our minds renewed. We need to be regularly called back to a vision of reality. Living out in the world, working every day among non-Christians, it is easy to be caught by the attitudes of the world around us. It is easy to get the idea that life should be a pleasant picnic, and that we should work toward the day when we can retire and just enjoy ourselves. This attitude is prevalent everywhere, but it is not what the Bible teaches.

The Bible says we are in the midst of a battle, a battle to the death against a keen and crafty foe. He wants to discourage us and defeat us, and he knows how to do it and never lets up. This life is not designed for relaxing. At times we need recreation and vacations to slow us down a bit, but you never see the apostle Paul talking about quitting the battle. We must not quit as long as we are alive. So Paul tells us we need to be reminded, day by day and week by week, of the battle we're in and the crafty foe we face. This life is a training ground where we are to learn our lessons, preparing us for the real thing yet to come.

A Priestly Ministry

The second thing the apostle said the Christians at Rome needed was a priestly ministry. He told them, "You not only need to be reminded of the truth, but you need an example to follow. You need somebody you can see doing this kind of thing. This is what God has given me the privilege of doing. I have been called by God into this ministry, not only to be an example of leadership, but also to be like a priest working in the temple, to awaken among you a sense of worship, a sense of the greatness of God." We need this frequently. I know I do, and I know you do too. From time to time we become dead inside. Despite all the exciting things happening, despite the tremendous encouragement on every side, at times we need to lift our eyes from our circumstances and stand before the greatness of God and see who it is we have to deal with, the One who is working through us. Paul did this and he is an example to us.

An Acceptable Offering

The third thing they needed, Paul says, is to "become an offering acceptable to God, sanctified by the Holy Spirit." Every congregation needs this. We need to labor, to pray, to work, to counsel, to evangelize. But all the activity of the Christian life is of no avail if it is not sanctified by the Holy Spirit. It must have in it the touch of God, that unction from on high, that divine wind blowing upon the dead bones and making them come to life. Paul is reminding the Roman Christians here of the ministry of prayer, and the need to remember God himself must touch something—otherwise it is dead and useless. So Paul calls the church at Rome back to this tremendous reality. They had so much, but they needed this as well.

Now we have reached a fantastic passage in which, for the first time in this letter, we get a close look at this mighty apostle himself. Did you ever stop to ask yourself what influence the apostle Paul has had in your own life? He lived nearly two thousand years ago, and yet not one person among us has not had his life drastically affected by him. The whole course of history has been changed by the truths he taught. In fact, for the most part, history itself has been built around the letters, teachings, doctrine, and ministry of the apostle Paul. We would not even be here, for America as a nation would not exist if this man had never lived. Even today we feel the freshness of his spirit, the greatness of his mind, and the fullness of his heart.

Paul tells us three things about his own ministry in this last section—the principles he worked under, the practice by which he carried them out, and a word about the power that he relied upon.

> *Therefore I glory in Christ Jesus in my service to God. I will not venture to speak of anything except what Christ has accomplished through me in leading the Gentiles to obey God by what I have said and done—by the power of signs and miracles, through the power of the Spirit. So from*

> *Jerusalem all the way around to Illyricum, I*
> *have fully proclaimed the gospel of Christ. It has*
> *always been my ambition to preach the gospel*
> *where Christ was not known, so that I would not*
> *be building on someone else's foundation (15:17-*
> *20).*

Concerning the principles of his ministry, Paul tells us four things. First, everywhere he went he found himself rejoicing. He said, "I rejoice, I glory in Christ Jesus, in my service to God." Why? Because when this man came into a city, he usually found it in the grip of Roman authority, ruled with an iron hand. He would find the people in widespread despair, empty and longing for something they could not find, fallen into degrading habits that were destroying homes and the very fabric of society itself. They were in the grip of superstitious fears. No church existed when he came, but after he had preached to them a while, light began to spring up in the darkness. People were changed; they began to live for the first time. They discovered why they were made, and excitement appeared in their lives. This happened everywhere Paul went, and it made him rejoice.

What God Has Done

Second, Paul gives us the secret of this kind of ministry.

> *I will not venture to speak of anything except*
> *what Christ has accomplished through me in*
> *leading the Gentiles to obey God by what I have*
> *said and done (15:18).*

This is the greatest secret God has to teach us: Man was designed not to do something to make God happy, but to let God work through the man. God would do the work. This is what Paul said—"what Christ has accomplished through me."

Not a week goes by but half a dozen posters and pamphlets cross my desk promoting the work of some man, telling me how much he has done for God. I have learned to throw most of them into the wastebasket unopened. But you never hear Paul telling how much he has done for God. Everywhere it is how much God has done through him. This is the secret of a truly effective life.

It took the apostle ten years to learn this secret. Like many young Christians, he started out with great zeal and desire to turn the world upside down, and he thought he had the equipment and gifts to do it. It took God ten years to show him that his brilliant mind, his mighty gifts, and his great personality, influence, and contacts were of no value in serving God. All God wanted was the man himself; he would work through him. When Paul learned this secret, he launched upon this great ministry that changed the history of the world.

Recently a young man asked me, "Why did God punish King David for numbering Israel?" This is one of the puzzles of the Old Testament. Why did God severely punish the king and his people when he took a census of Israel? It does not sound like a very serious crime, does it? But it represented David's departure from the principle of dependence upon God to be his resource, and a shift to the world's resource of numbers. Nothing has contributed more to the weakness of the church than this dependence upon numbers, as though a great crowd of people can do something. When you meet one person willing to trust God to work through him, there is no limit to what God can do. This is the secret of Paul's ministry.

Third, he tells us of its power—"by the power of signs and miracles, through the power of the Spirit" (15:19). These signs and miracles were the signs of an apostle. Paul tells us in 2 Corinthians that wherever he went he performed signs and wonders. Many people ask why we can't perform these signs today. The answer is that they were the mark of an apostle and only apostles did these things. Today we do not need more apostles; we have the writings of the original ones available to us. We also have what Paul mentions, the power of the Spirit and His impact on human lives.

The Corinthians once had the nerve to write Paul and ask, "The next time you show up in Corinth, how about bringing a letter of recommendation from Peter and James and John?" Paul wrote back and said, "Do you really mean that? Don't you understand that *you* are my letter of recommendation? Look at what's happened in your lives: You used to be drunkards and homosexuals and thieves and murderers—'such were some of you!' But what are you now? Look at the change! You are all the letter of recommendation I need." Paul's life and ministry were constantly characterized by the display of the power of God to change lives.

Then finally, look at how widespread his ministry was:

> *So from Jerusalem all the way around to Illyricum, I have fully proclaimed the gospel of Christ (15:19).*

You really must have a map to see this. Jerusalem is way down on the eastern corner of the Mediterranean Sea, in Asia. Paul had traveled up and down the coast, on into what we call Turkey, in Asia Minor, up across the Dardanelles into Europe, then into

Macedonia and Greece. He had gone, as he tells us here, into Illyricum, now called Yugoslavia. The nature of his ministry was pioneering:

> *It has always been my ambition to preach the gospel where Christ was not known (15:20).*

He never wanted to build on another man's work. I believe this is characteristic of the Spirit of God. He loves to thrust out into new areas. We are to reach out with the good news, as Paul did.

Planning Perspective

Now for a paragraph on how he practiced this ministry:

> *This is why I have often been hindered from coming to you. But now that there is no more place for me to work in these regions, and since I have been longing for many years to see you, I plan to do so when I go to Spain. I hope to visit you while passing through and to have you assist me on my journey there, after I have enjoyed your company for a while (15:22-24).*

Here is Paul's word about how practical his ministry was. He tells us *first* that it involved planning for the future. I am always running into Christians who think God gives his orders directly to them while they are moving. They think of the Christian life as going on automatic pilot where they float around, waiting for orders as they go. They never think of planning or looking ahead. But Paul did not live like this.

For many years he had longed to go to Spain, and he planned to do so. But notice something about his planning. First, it was flexible; he did not have a timetable. He went according to the way God opened the doors, but he planned to go in a certain direction, which he kept clearly in mind. He did not tell God how or when it had to be. This is Christian planning.

Second, he was persistent; he did not give up. He had set his heart on Rome and Spain, and he was going there. No matter how long it took, he kept plodding steadily toward the goal. We don't know whether Paul ever got to Spain, though Scripture hints he undertook a fourth missionary journey after he wrote the letters to Timothy. In any event, Spain was the focus of his heart's desire.

The *third* thing about Paul's planning was that it always involved a team. He never went alone, and he says to these Romans, "When I come, I expect you to help me go on"—perhaps to supply some assistance, some money, and to pray as he went. Paul never worked independently, as a prima donna; he always involved others.

The second factor about his ministry is found in verse 25 and following:

> *Now, however, I am on my way to Jerusalem in the service of the saints there. For Macedonia and Achaia were pleased to make a contribution for the poor among the saints in Jerusalem. They were pleased to do it, and indeed they owe it to them. For if the Gentiles have shared in the Jews' spiritual blessings, they owe it to the Jews to share with them their material blessings. So after I have completed this task and have made sure that they have received this fruit, I will go to Spain and visit you on the way. I know that when I come to you, I will come in the full measure of the blessing of Christ (15:25-29).*

Now, not only was Paul practical enough to plan, but he also fulfilled past commitments. Some

Christians, I find, are forever jumping into new things before finishing the old. But Paul did not do this. Many years before this, in the council at Jerusalem (Acts 15), Paul and Barnabas were sent to Antioch with a letter to the church, settling the question of circumcision for the Gentiles. In the letter Paul was specifically asked to be careful to remember the poor. Now, many years later, he is still fulfilling this requirement. He has taken up an offering every place he has gone, and now he wants to deliver it personally to the famine-stricken saints in Jerusalem and Judea.

It is not beneath the apostle to give material help. He is not going up to preach to these people, but to help them with material things. Christianity involves both emphases—spiritual and physical. Paul was willing to take up offerings and personally carry the money to those in need. But here he gives us the principle of sharing:

> For if the Gentiles have shared in the Jews' spiritual blessings, they owe it to the Jews to share with them their material blessings (15:27).

If someone blesses you spiritually, and the only way you can thank him is with material things, then do it, Paul says. This is God's program, to give back in material things for the spiritual blessings you have received. Notice he says, "after I have completed this task . . . ." He is not going to quit until he is through. He will wrap it up well and do it right. "When I have made sure they have received this fruit, then I will go to Spain and visit you on the way."

The third aspect of the practical character of Paul's ministry is his trust in the power of God:

> I know that when I come to you, I will come in the full measure of the blessing of Christ (15:29).

He counted on God to come through. This introduces the last paragraph, where he touches on the power of his ministry:

> *I urge you, brothers, by our Lord Jesus Christ and by the love of the Spirit, to join me in my struggle by praying to God for me. Pray that I may be rescued from the unbelievers in Judea and that my service in Jerusalem may be acceptable to the saints there, so that by God's will I may come to you with joy and together with you be refreshed. The God of peace be with you all. Amen (15:30-33).*

What was behind this mighty apostle's ministry? Why has it lasted for two thousand years? What was it that opened the doors and gave him access even into Caesar's household, and before the throne of the emperor himself? Paul would tell you it was the prayers of God's people for him. He was well aware of the power of prayer, and he urges them to pray.

To Honor the Lord Jesus

Here we have a brief word on the nature of prayer. What is the basis of it? "I urge you, brothers, by our Lord Jesus Christ and by the love of the Spirit . . . ." Prayer is born of the Spirit of God within us, awakening a desire to help, a sense of love and compassion. And the reason we pray is to honor the Lord Jesus. When people see the honor of Christ involved, and the love of the Spirit fulfilled by prayer, they will really begin to pray. Paul says, "Join me in my struggle." Life is a struggle, and Paul sees prayer as a way of fighting in the combat. It is a great weapon that can batter down doors and open others. It can remove obstacles, withstand tremendous pressure and forces, and uphold and sustain people.

Notice what Paul requested his readers to pray: for protection from the unbelievers, and for acceptance by the saints. These are two areas where Satan loves to attack. If he can lay a person low with physical illness, or spiritual attack, he will do so. Prayer is particularly powerful at this point; it can protect someone in danger. After Paul arrived in Jerusalem, as we learn from the book of Acts, he was set upon by a mob in the temple courts. They were out to kill him right on the spot. They had rocks in their hands and were going to stone him to death. But at this critical moment, the commander of the Roman legion on the other side of the wall, in the castle of Antonia, looked over into the temple court and saw what was going on. He came down with a band of soldiers and rescued the apostle in the nick of time. So prayer was answered, and Paul was protected from the unbelievers.

Earlier in Acts, Luke tells us, when Paul came with his gift, many Christians in Jerusalem of Jewish background did not want to accept Paul. They regarded him as a renegade, a traitor to the Jewish cause. They were turning their backs on him. But James, in answer to prayer, interfered. He asked Paul to take on a certain commitment to demonstrate to the people that he was not against the law. This turned the tide, and Paul's ministry was accepted. Thus Paul's prayer requests were honored and God gave him what they asked.

Finally, Paul gives us his personal expectation of the results of their prayers:

> *By God's will I may come to you with joy and together with you be refreshed (15:32).*

The book of Acts closes three years from this time, with Paul finally arriving in Rome after undergoing shipwreck and arduous travels. On his way to the capital, in a place called the Three Taverns, he was met by a delegation of Christians from the city. What an encouragement they must have been to the apostle, who was coming as a prisoner chained to a Roman guard, on trial for his life, and waiting to appear before the emperor. They refreshed his heart and spirit.

I hope this review of Paul's ministry will remind you we are in a battle and we cannot take time out. We have to maintain the task and be faithful to what God has called us to do. Above everything else, we must seek the mighty unction of the Holy Spirit on all that happens. It must not be just a mechanical process, but the power of God released among us.

16
ALL IN
THE FAMILY

(Romans 16:1-24)

Many ignore Romans 16 because they see in it nothing but a list of names of people long since dead and gone. But in many ways this is one of the most exciting chapters in Romans, as I think you will see.

Something in all of us wants to see our names preserved. Years ago I visited the Natural Bridge of Virginia. Hundreds of names and initials were scratched on the rocks, but high on one side of it, above almost every other name, was scratched "George Washington." Even the father of our country felt the urge to gain a kind of immortality by carving his name on the rock.

But here in Romans 16 is a list of names of men and women who never knew they were going to be famous. If they had known a mention in one of Paul's letters would give them undying fame, a long line of people might have been outside his door urging him to include them in the letter. But these names are mentioned only because they were personal friends of Paul's in Rome, or they were with him in the city of Corinth where the letter was written.

In this chapter, the names of thirty-three people are mentioned. Nine of them were with Paul—eight men and one woman. Twenty-four were in Rome—seventeen men and seven women. Two households are mentioned, and two unnamed women—the mother of Rufus and the sister of Nereus—as well as some unnamed brethren. So the apostle knew personally quite a number of people in Rome though he himself had not yet visited the city. He had met them somewhere else in the empire. We tend to think of these ancient days as a time of limited travel, and they were. It took weeks to reach cities we now reach in less than an hour by plane. Nevertheless, these people got around, and here is proof.

This passage has three simple divisions. First, Paul's greetings to the brothers and sisters at Rome (the first sixteen verses); then a brief warning about phony Christians in Rome; and finally, greetings from the brothers who were with Paul as he wrote.

The letter to the Romans was carried by a traveling businesswoman, Phoebe, who is introduced to us in the chapter's opening verses:

> *I commend to you our sister Phoebe, a servant of the church in Cenchrea. I ask you to receive her in the Lord in a way worthy of the saints and to give her any help she may need from you, for she has been a great help to many people, including me (16:1-2).*

The whole church can be grateful to this woman for her faithfulness. She bore and preserved this letter throughout the hazardous journey from Corinth to Rome. She is called by the apostle "a servant of the church in Cenchrea." Cenchrea was a port of Corinth, located about nine miles east of the city. Evidently a Christian church had grown up there, and Phoebe was a deacon in it. (This is really the term, not "deaconness," as the Revised Standard Version puts it; the word is the same for male or female.) This does not mean she held some governmental office in the church, however. We sometimes read present day meanings into these words. It means she had assumed a ministry on behalf of the church. She represented them in some labor, and whether it was material, physical, or spiritual, she was faithful in it. So Paul commends her to these Christians in Rome and asks them not only to receive her but to help her. "She has been a help to many others," he says, "and to me."

You cannot read Romans 16 without being impressed by the number of women Paul mentions—many more than in any other literature of that day. Women occupy a prominent place in these letters of the New Testament. They handled important tasks within the church, according to their gifts. There is a strong suggestion here that Phoebe was a teacher or an evangelist—a laborer for the gospel with Paul. We do not know much more about her, but her name has been preserved forever because of this mention.

A Church in Their Home

Paul now turns to greet those he knew in Rome, and he begins with a well-known husband-and-wife team:

> *Greet Priscilla and Aquila, my fellow workers in Christ Jesus. They risked their lives for me.*

Not only I but all the churches of the Gentiles are
grateful to them. Greet also the church that meets
at their house (16:3-5).

We meet this couple first in Acts 18, where Luke
tells us they were Jews, tentmakers by trade, who
were driven out of Rome by the decree of the Emperor
Claudius in 52 A.D. They went to Corinth, took up
their trade there, and met this strange young Jew,
also a tentmaker, who had come from the north. Saul
of Tarsus apparently moved in with them and soon
led them to Christ. Theirs was probably the first
home in Corinth to hold a church. Luke tells us that
after two years there, Paul left to go to the great city
of Ephesus, and Priscilla and Aquila went with him.
Again they took up the tentmaking trade and again
opened up a church in their home.

They also ministered in the synagogue in Ephesus,
for Luke tells us that one morning they heard a
mighty and eloquent man named Apollos preaching.
But it was evident to them he did not understand the
fullness of the gospel, for he preached only what John
the Baptist taught, that "One was coming, who
would do mighty things." After the service they in-
vited him home to dinner (a wonderful thing to do
for a preacher!) and instructed him more fully. Because of their service to him, Apollos went on to
Corinth where he had a mighty ministry in the word
of God. Incidentally, of the six times their names are
mentioned, four times Priscilla's name is put first—
which might indicate she rather than her husband
had the gift of teaching.

Now they are in Rome, having traveled from
Corinth and Ephesus. Paul greets them and reminds
the church they had risked their lives for him. He was
referring probably to the uproar that broke out in
Ephesus, recorded in Acts 19, when the whole city

was upset and a mob was intent on taking Paul's life. He writes that everywhere this couple went they had a church in their home.

In these early days Christians did not meet in buildings like we have now. In fact, in the first three hundred years of church history no church buildings are mentioned. What a relief not to be bothered with a building program! People got together where they could for larger meetings. In Rome, Christians gathered in at least three (and probably many more) house churches, one of them in the home of Priscilla and Aquila.

Paul goes on to mention two other friends:

> *Greet my dear friend Epenetus, who was the first convert to Christ in the province of Asia. Greet Mary, who worked very hard for you (16:5-6).*

Epenetus was never forgotten, for he was the first one to believe the gospel when Paul came to the province of Asia, of which Ephesus was the capital. You never forget the first one you lead to Christ. No matter how many others follow, you never forget the first fruits. We do not know what Epenetus was doing in Rome but he was cherished because he was the first to exercise faith in Asia. Associated with him is Mary, whom Paul calls "Mary the toiler." She is one of the group of unknown women in the Gospels who had the gift of helps. She could not teach or preach or evangelize, but she could work, and she did. Paul is very careful to remember these women and men who had the gift of helps.

Friends and Relatives

Then he mentions some relatives and friends:

> *Greet Andronicus and Junias, my relatives who have been in prison with me. They are*

outstanding among the apostles, and they were in
Christ before I was. Greet Ampliatus, whom I
love in the Lord. Greet Urbanus, our fellow
worker in Christ, and my dear friend Stachys.
Greet Apelles, tested and approved in Christ
(16:7-10).

Andronicus and Junias were relatives of Paul, and
since he says they were "in Christ before me," this
takes us back to the very first days of the church, back
to the ministry of Stephen in Jerusalem. What it
must have meant to the young Saul of Tarsus, who
was breathing out threats of slaughter against the
Christians there, to learn that two of his own
kinsmen had become Christians! Undoubtedly the
prayers of Andronicus and Junias affected the apostle.

It is hard to tell whether this is a husband-and-wife
team or two brothers. It all depends on the name
"Junias." If it is "Junias" with an "s," as we have it
here, it is a male; if "Junia," as the King James Version has it, it is female. But whoever they were, they
were Jewish relatives of Paul who had become Christians. With this wistful note Paul remembers they
were in Christ before him; no doubt they were praying for him. Somewhere along the line they shared a
term with him in prison; what better place to develop
friendships—there is no escaping your fellow in-
mates! They became Paul's fast friends as well as his
relatives, and Paul speaks highly of them. He says
even the twelve apostles in Jerusalem held them in
high regard. What they were doing in Rome we do
not know. Doubtless they were leaders in the church
there.

Ampliatus is an interesting name. In the cemetery
of Domitilla among the catacombs in Rome is a
highly decorated tomb with the single name

"Ampliatus" written on it. A single name like this implies the man was a slave, but as the tomb is rather ornate, it indicates he was a Christian and highly respected by the leaders in Rome. We cannot be sure it was the same person Paul mentions here, but most likely it is. This man, though a slave, had a great ministry among the brethren in Rome.

We know no more about Urbanus and Stachys than what Paul mentions here. Somewhere, Urbanus joined Paul's team, and also "his dear friend Stachys." But I have always been fascinated by this man Apelles, whom Paul says has been "tested and approved in Christ." (I would love to have that inscription on my tombstone!) This man will forever be known as the one who endured a testing of his faith and who stood against the pressure. Thus he has been approved in Christ. His name means "called," and he certainly proved himself to be one whom God had called.

Christians in High Places

In the latter part of verse 10 and in verse 11 two groups are mentioned, involving Christians and perhaps non-Christians as well.

> Greet those who belong to the household of Aristobulus. Greet Herodion, my relative. Greet those in the household of Narcissus who are in the Lord.

Dr. William Barclay, probably the best commentator of all in getting at the background of biblical stories, tells us that Aristobulus may have been the grandson of King Herod the Great, who lived in Rome. He was behind the scenes politically, but was a close friend of the Emperor Claudius. When Aristobulus died, his household, that is, his servants and slaves, became the property of the emperor but was still known as the household of Aristobulus. This is probably the group Paul is referring to. If so, it means a number of Christian servants and slaves were in the royal household, exercising great influence on Rome's leaders—even upon the emperor himself. This is supported by the fact that Paul mentions his relative Herodion in connection with these servants. From his name we see this man had connections with the family of Herod. This is also a hint to us that Paul himself had a connection with the ruling family of the Jews.

The most famous Narcissus we know in Roman history was a former slave who became the personal secretary of the Emperor Claudius. He gained much wealth because he was in charge of the emperor's correspondence, and his palm had to be greased before a letter could get through to the emperor. When Claudius was murdered, Nero took over, and he also took over the household of Narcissus. Shortly after Nero came to the throne he forced Narcissus and many other men to commit suicide. From this mention in Romans 16, Christians were clearly among his household: "Greet those in the household of Narcissus who are in the Lord." In the heart of the Roman Empire, a Christian witness already had been established.

Next we get another band of hard-working ladies:

Greet Tryphena and Tryphosa, those women who work hard in the Lord. Greet my dear friend Persis, another woman who has worked very hard in the Lord. Greet Rufus, chosen in the Lord, and his mother, who has been a mother to me, too (16:12-13).

These words of Paul's open up hidden vistas and bring the whole flavor and color of this first-century Christian life home to us. Here were Tryphaena and Tryphosa, these dear maiden sisters who worked very hard. There is a delicate irony here. When Paul wrote this he probably smiled to himself, for their names mean "dainty" and "delicate"—yet they were hard workers. Their names suggest nobility, and perhaps they were born to aristocracy. And yet, they who did not have to work for a livelihood worked hard in the service of the Lord.

We know nothing about Paul's dear friend Persis, other than that she too had worked with him somewhere, perhaps traveling in his company of evangelists.

In verse 13 we have Rufus, chosen in the Lord, and his mother, who had been a mother to the apostle, too. There seems to be little doubt that Rufus, along with his brother Alexander (mentioned in the Gospel of Mark), were the sons of Simon of Cyrene. In the gospels we are told that as our Lord was making his way down the Via Dolorosa in Jerusalem on his way to the cross, he was so weak from loss of blood he tripped and fell. The Roman soldiers laid hold of a passing stranger whom they compelled to bear the cross to Calvary. That man was Simon of Cyrene, a Jew coming into the city for the Passover. His home was in North Africa, and he evidently had little or no interest in the things of Christ until he was forced to carry the cross of Jesus. Though we do not know the details, this man evidently became a Christian, and the book of Acts hints he was present on the day of Pentecost.

His two sons, Alexander and Rufus, became outstanding men in the Christian community. There is an Alexander who comes to the rescue of Paul in the city of Ephesus, at the time of the outcry there. There is a Rufus here in Rome, who is well-known, and Paul sends his greetings to him, and reminds him also that Rufus's mother had been his mother too at some time. Back in the earliest days of the gospel ministry young Saul of Tarsus, coming to Jerusalem to sit at the feet of Gamaliel, the great Jewish teacher, had probably stayed in the home of Simon of Cyrene and his two sons, Alexander and Rufus. Later they became Christians, and Paul cherished them as friends he had known even before his own Christian days.

In verse 14 we find a businessmen's group:

> Greet Asyncritus, Phlegon, Hermes, Patrobas, Hermas and the brothers with them.

Here, possibly, is a kind of male commune, all with Greek names. These may have been young businessmen who had come to Rome and formed a house church in their bachelors' quarters. Paul sends his greetings to them and all the brothers with them.

Then a final group, perhaps another house church in Rome:

> Greet Philologus, Julia, Nereus and his sister, and Olympas and all the saints with them. Greet one another with a holy kiss. All the churches of Christ send greetings (15-16).

Philologus means "a lover of the word," and this was probably a nickname given to him, just as Barnabas was called "the son of consolation," though this was not his name. Here was a man who loved the Word of God, and gathered with him these men and women—Julia, Nereus and his sister.

Nereus is another fascinating name. Dr. Barclay suggests he may have been housekeeper for a prominent Roman citizen named Flavius Clemens—later to become consul, the city's highest political office—who in 95 A.D. was condemned to death by Emperor Domitian because he was a Christian. His wife, Domatilla, also a Christian, was banished by the emperor. We can see from these names that Roman society already had been infiltrated by the gospel. This is why Paul says at the beginning of this letter, "Your faith is being reported all over the world." These prominent Christians had already penetrated society from top to bottom. This is the way Christianity should work. It makes its best progress when it infiltrates all levels of society and brings them together in the church of Christ.

Divisive Forces

Now we have a warning paragraph, indicating Paul is thinking of his own trip to Jerusalem and the threat awaiting him from the Judaizers there:

> *I urge you, brothers, to watch out for those who cause divisions and put obstacles in your way that are contrary to the teaching you have learned. Keep away from them. For such people are not serving our Lord Christ, but their own appetites. By smooth talk and flattery they deceive the minds of naive people. Everyone has heard about your obedience, so I am full of joy over you; but I want you to be wise about what is good, and innocent about what is evil (16:17-19).*

This is a helpful passage on what to do about problems within the church. Here is a group of professing Christians, but who (to judge by the apostle's language) are not truly believers. The danger, as Paul outlines it, is that they create factions within a church—little dissident groups emphasizing one particular point of doctrine to the exclusion of everything else. This is always a problem within the church when people think one particular thing is most important. We have people today who emphasize tongues, or prophecy, or some phase of teaching they think is the mark of a true believer, to the exclusion of everything else. Paul warns about this.

The second thing they do is to introduce practices or ceremonies that Paul calls "obstacles to faith," certain rituals or practices that these groups insist are the marks of true Christianity. They build a sense of superiority in their devotees. They say, "If you have this mark, then you really are a Christian." Their motives, Paul says, are not to serve Christ, even though they say they do. These factions are really out to advance themselves, to get a following, to gain prestige. You can tell what they want by the way they act. Their methods are to come on with smooth and plausible talk. They always use scriptural language, and appear to be the most dedicated and devoted of believers. Have you noticed how many cults today are trying to go back to the Scriptures, arguing from them a groundwork for their teachings?

Another method is flattery. They make Christians feel important. They lift them up and flatter them by giving them a peculiar mark of distinction: members of the "true" church. Such methods always cause division. When some group like this appears many want to rush in and excommunicate them, read them out of the church from the pulpit, or violently attack them. Paul does not say to do any of those things. His advice is to keep away from them. Ignore them! "You Christians in Rome have a reputation for obedience. You have a spirit of wanting to obey what the Lord says. Now here is your word from the Lord: Do not follow them. Do not get involved with these separatist groups. The God of peace, who will preserve the peace of the church, will also crush Satan under your feet." If you keep away from these groups something will happen to open people's eyes to their unscriptural position, and they will lose their following. Peace will be preserved without a lot of warfare and dissension.

In verses 21-23 we have the greetings of those who are with Paul in Corinth:

> *Timothy, my fellow worker, sends his greetings to you, as do Lucius, Jason and Sosipater, my relatives. I, Tertius, who wrote down this letter, greet you in the Lord. Gaius, whose hospitality I and the whole church here enjoy, sends you his greetings. Erastus, who is the city's director of public works, and our brother Quartus send you their greetings.*

This brings us to the final paragraph when, as was his custom, Paul takes his pen and writes the last words himself. Up to this point he has been dictating this letter to a man who identifies himself in verse 22: "I, Tertius, who wrote down this letter, greet you in the Lord." The apostle must have said something to him, such as, "Tertius, you've written this whole thing and you must have writer's cramp by now. Just write another line and send your own greetings." The name indicates he was a slave, because his name means "Third." In slave families they did not bother to think up names; they just numbered the children. First, Second, Third, Fourth, Fifth, and so on. Here are Third and Fourth of a family of slaves. (His brother Quartus, Fourth, is mentioned in verse 23.)

They are educated slaves who have become Christians. These men can read and write, and are part of this group in Corinth.

You can picture them gathered in the home of Gaius, the gracious, genial, generous host of the city, who is also mentioned in Paul's first letter to the Corinthians. Gaius opened his house to the entire Christian community. So here is Paul, sitting with his friends. Tertius is writing down the letter, and the others are gathered around listening to Paul as he dictates, profiting much from the writing of these great truths. Also there is Paul's dear son in the faith, Timothy, whom we know so well from the two letters addressed to him. Paul always spoke of him in the highest terms: his beloved son in the faith, who had stayed with him so long and remained faithful to the end. The very last letter Paul wrote from his prison cell in Rome was to Timothy.

Paul also mentions Lucius, Jason, and Sosipater, his relatives. Here in Romans 16 are mentioned six members of Paul's family, kinsmen who are now Christians. Some were Christians before him, but some Paul influenced toward Christ. They come from various places. Lucius appears to be the same one who comes from Cyrene, mentioned in chapter 13 of Acts as one of the teachers in the city of Antioch. Jason was evidently Paul's host when the apostle went to the city of Thessalonica in Macedonia. Paul stayed in Jason's home when a riot broke out in the city. Sosipater may be the man from Berea mentioned in Acts 20:9 as Sopater, whom Paul met in Macedonia and accompanied to Jerusalem with the offering to the churches there.

The final name is Erastus, director of public works in the city of Corinth. You can see how the gospel penetrated all levels of society, with slaves, public officials, consuls, and leaders of the empire, all sharing an equal ground of fellowship in the church of Jesus Christ.

Faithful Commitment

The Christians in this list were noted for their steady, tested commitment, their faithfulness to the gospel. I am troubled today when I see Christians succumbing so easily to the world's philosophy of life: Live for your own pleasure, try to retire as early as possible so you can do as little as you can. This is a deadly philosophy, and the early Christians did not believe it.

Four things ring clearly throughout their lives:

First, *they were not their own.* They believed the truth Paul wrote about in 1 Corinthians 6:19-20— "You are not your own; you are bought with a price." They knew they did not have a right to direct their lives any longer. God had sent them into the world, and God would take them through it.

Second, *they believed life is a battle to the death.* It is not a picnic. They expected to be engaged in never-ending warfare until they left this life, so they kept on fighting.

Third, *they believed in the need for rest and leisure at times, but only to restore them to go back into the battle.*

Finally, *they understood that the gifts of the Holy Spirit among them opened up a ministry for every single believer.* No Christian was without a ministry. Those who could not teach or preach could still help—and they did, right to the end. Surely this passage reminds us that God has called us all to a ministry, and we all have to give an account for what we have done with our gifts. We had better find out what they are and get to work, because God has placed us not on a picnic ground, but a battleground.

17
THE GREAT
MYSTERY

(Romans 16:25-27)

Now we have come to the very last paragraph of the letter to the Romans. At this point Paul probably took the pen and wrote the final words in his own hand. He tells us in 2 Thessalonians it was his custom to do this—to protect his letters from forgery, for one thing—but also to bear a personal greeting to those to whom he was writing. Almost all scholars agree the apostle probably suffered from a serious eye problem, as the letter to the Galatians suggests. So Paul wrote these marvelous words in large letters with his own hand:

Now to him who is able to establish you by my gospel and the proclamation of Jesus Christ,

*according to the revelation of the mystery hidden
for long ages past, but now revealed and made
known through the prophetic writings by the command of the eternal God, so that all nations
might believe and obey him—to the only wise
God be glory forever through Jesus Christ! Amen
(16:25-27).*

Those remarkable words constitute a summary of
the whole letter—a beautiful finale to this great
epistle. Notice the goal of the apostle is to establish
the readers of his letter. Have you ever had the desire
to be established? Many people think they are established when actually they are simply stuck in the
mud! Most of us think being established means the
end of all progress; we sit down, camp there, and
that's it. In this sense, many Christians are established. But when Paul speaks of our being established
he means standing on solid, stable ground, both doctrinally and in experience.

Have you ever moved a picnic table to a shadier
spot and tried to find a place where all four legs
touched the ground at the same time? You tried to
establish it so it would not rock or become shaky.
This is the idea Paul has in mind in this word "establish." God wants to bring you and me to a place
where we are no longer rocking or shaky or unstable,
but solid and secure. The idea is basically what all
human beings look for: an inner security from which
you can handle all the problems of life. You become
dependable, and have a true sense of worth, so nothing gets to you or shakes you up or throws you off
balance.

The One Who Is Able

Notice the resource the apostle counts on to make
this happen: "Now to him who is able to establish

you . . . ." God himself is responsible for this. You and I are not given final responsibility to bring this about. Isn't that encouraging? Now there are things God asks us to do: We are to understand what he is saying to us in this letter and we are to cooperate with him and give ourselves to these things. But even if we do not, Paul is saying, we do not have the ultimate responsibility to bring this about. God will do it.

As the apostle wrote this, I'm sure he had in mind all the instances and circumstances from the past that are given to us in the Old Testament to encourage us. God established Abraham, who was an idol worshiper. Abraham could not tell the truth about his wife. Twice he lied about her because he thought it would save him from difficulty. Though Abraham had various character faults, God stabilized him, established him, and brought him to a place where he became one of the great names of all time.

God also did this with Moses and David, and of course with Paul himself. Paul was a brilliant young Jew with an ambitious heart, a sharp mind, and a strong sense of achievement, due to his notable gifts and his desire to become famous. Yet God broke him, softened him, changed him, and put him through circumstances he did not understand at the time. Finally he was established, so that no matter what came he remained strong, steady, trusting, and certain. This is the great good news of this letter. God is able to establish you.

Paul goes on to tell us three things God will use during this process. *First* he says, "Now to him who is able to establish you *by my gospel* . . . ." Paul does not mean he has a unique gospel. Unfortunately some teachers have taken these words in this way, and have concluded the apostle Paul was given a special revelation no one else possessed—one that Peter, James, John, and other writers of Scripture did not know. This teaching has been widespread among certain men of our day and many have followed it, but it is not what Paul means. He answered this accusation in 1 Corinthians when he said, in effect, "Some of you are following me, some are following Apollos, and some are following Cephas, but this is wrong. We are not different; we all have the same gospel. You are making too much of men. The message is always the same." He rebuked them for tending to divide and to follow certain leaders and teachers.

A Unique Revelation

Paul means he was given a unique revelation of this gospel. You find this in 1 Corinthians 11: "For I received from the Lord what I also passed on to you: The Lord Jesus, on the night he was betrayed, took bread, and when he had given thanks, he broke it and said, 'This is my body, which is for you . . . .'" Paul is saying, "I was not there at the Lord's supper. I was not even a Christian then. I have not talked with Peter or James or John about this, and none of the men who were present told me what happened in that room. I know what happened because Jesus himself appeared to me and told me. I have told you only what I received from the Lord himself." The Lord taught Paul the same gospel the other apostles believed, and this is what Paul means when he says "according to my gospel."

The practical impact of this phrase upon us is this: the test of all true Christian messages is that they must be in line with the apostolic writings. The apostles tell us the truth about the gospel. This is why today we must always check any teaching or

practice that claims to be Christian and see if it fits
with what the apostles gave us. Paul says this is what
God will use to establish you: "My gospel, that which
was given to me."

The *second* element is the proclamation of Jesus
Christ. Here Paul unfolds to us the heart of his gospel. Paul was a mighty theologian; there has never
been a greater. Sometimes when I visit seminaries I
am tempted to say to the young men and women
studying there, "Why waste your time with these
fourth-rate theologians of today, when you could be
spending your time with first-rate theologians—
Peter, James, John, and Paul?" Theology was not the
heart of Paul's gospel, however. The heart of his gospel was the revelation of a Person, Jesus himself. All
through the letter Paul has emphasized this fact again
and again: everything centers in Christ. He is the
heart of it all. Therefore a gospel that leaves out
Christ is a phony gospel.

Jesus himself declared the uniqueness of his position: "I am the way, the truth, and the life. No man
comes to the Father except by me." In the whole
realm of theology no one is like Jesus Christ. In all
the history of the religions of the world, no one is
equal to him, or can be remotely compared to him.
Therefore any gospel that minimizes Christ or puts
him on the level of other names is a perversion of the
true gospel of Jesus Christ. Christ is the central figure
of all history, of all time, of all faith.

The Mystery Revealed

There is a *third* element, the apostle says, which
has been the theme throughout Romans, although it
is not always presented in the same terms. Paul says,
"God will use not only my gospel and the

proclamation of Jesus Christ, but he will also establish you by the explanation of the mystery"—

> *according to the revelation of the mystery hidden for long ages past, but now revealed and made known through the prophetic writings by the command of the eternal God, so that all nations might believe and obey him.*

The ultimate test of any Christian message is: Does it proclaim the mystery? There are thousands of places in this land today where people meet regularly in Christian churches. They sing the same hymns we sing, read the same Bible, and praise God in the same way. And yet in thousands and thousands of those churches nothing exciting is happening, nothing reaches out and touches the community. Do you know why? Because the mystery is not being proclaimed. Here is the heart of the gospel, this amazing mystery. The question we need to ask about any church is, "Does it teach men and women to live on the basis of this fantastic secret, once hidden but now fully revealed?

What is this mystery? There are several references to it in the New Testament, sometimes referring to a part of it, sometimes referring to the whole. The only other reference to this mystery in the letter to the Romans is found in 11:25-26:

> *I do not want you to be ignorant of this mystery, brothers, so that you may not be conceited: Israel has experienced a hardening in part until the full number of the Gentiles has come in. And so all Israel will be saved, as it is written:*

This is part of the mystery. Paul says God intends to unite both Jews and Gentiles into one body. For this to happen, the Jews must be partially blinded for

a while to allow the Gentiles to see. This is what has
been going on for two thousand years of human history: a partial blindness in Israel. We do not understand fully what is involved here, but it seems necessary in God's program.

This aspect of the mystery is also referred to in
Ephesians 3:2-6:

> *Surely you have heard about the administration*
> *of God's grace that was given to me for you, that*
> *is, the mystery made known to me by revelation,*
> *as I have already written briefly. In reading this,*
> *then, you will be able to understand my insight*
> *into the mystery of Christ, which was not made*
> *known to men in other generations as it has now*
> *been revealed by the Spirit to God's holy apostles*
> *and prophets. This mystery is that through the*
> *gospel the Gentiles are heirs together with Israel,*
> *members together of one body, and sharers together*
> *in the promise in Christ Jesus.*

This is an extremely important part of the mystery. But these references to parts of the mystery are
not to be regarded as distinct and separate mysteries.
They are all one, as we will see. The heart of the mystery is given to us in Colossians 1:24-27, one of the
clearest statements of it:

> *Now I rejoice in what was suffered for you, and*
> *I fill up in my flesh what is still lacking in regard*
> *to Christ's afflictions, for the sake of his body,*
> *which is the church. I have become its servant by*
> *the commission God gave me to present to you the*
> *word of God in its fullness—the mystery that has*
> *been kept hidden for ages and generations, but is*
> *now disclosed to the saints. To them God has cho-*
> *sen to make known among the Gentiles the*

*glorious riches of this mystery, which is Christ in
you, the hope of glory."*

There is the mystery. All that God is, wrapped up
in a Person, and given to you and to me—the only
hope we have of ever discovering the glory God intended for us as human beings. Christ *in you*, the
hope of glory.

Another reference to the wonder of this mystery is
in 1 Timothy 3:16. Paul describes it in terms of a
hymn of the early church:

*Beyond all question, the mystery of godliness is
great:*

*He appeared in a body,
      was vindicated by the Spirit,
   was seen by angels,
      was preached among the nations,
   was believed on in the world,
      was taken up in glory.*

Jesus himself is the mystery. Through his virgin
birth, through his holy and sinless life, through his
substitutionary death upon a violent and cruel cross,
through his startling breakout from the prison of
death, and through the gift of the Holy Spirit on the
day of Pentecost, God has given Jesus—all he is and
all he has—to you and to me. This enables us to do
two things: to deny our natural abilities and
strengths, and to rely wholly on Jesus' ability and
strength—and thus to live our lives today as though
Jesus himself was living them. This is the mystery.
This is the radical, powerful secret of authentic
Christianity: Christ in you, the hope of glory.

Never Boring

Do you know this mystery? Do you know it not
only in your mind but in your experience? The

knowledge of it and the living of it turns Christianity into an exciting adventure. It may be demanding, it may even be scary, but I can guarantee you it will never be boring, because the mystery is at work. If you are filled with the secret, the indwelling of Christ, it does not make any difference if you are a Jew or a Gentile. All the divisions of class, sex, and national origin are eliminated by the secret. It does not make any difference whether you are rich or poor, slave or free. By this mystery, all are one in Christ Jesus.

Whenever a Christian lives on this basis, really trusting that God is in him through Jesus Christ to be his wisdom, his power, his strength; when he attempts things only on the basis of expecting God to fulfill his promise, and so he moves out to do things by God's grace, he finds himself "established." If you want a place of security, it won't come by your reckoning on what you can do for God. That will never work. It will depend on how much you believe God is ready to do through you.

Paul says two further things about this. First, though the results of this lifestyle were *experienced* by men and women of God in the Old Testament, no *explanation* was ever given there of how this happened. When you read the Old Testament you find men and women puzzled as to how God was going to put together all its great promises and themes. There is the promise of the restoration of Israel. There is also the promise of the forgiveness of an individual's sins. And there is the mighty promise of the healing of the nations and the cessation of war.

At last the process of fulfillment began to unfold: Jesus came. He was the secret. He would fulfill all the tremendous promises and themes of the Old Testament. The historic appearance of Jesus was required to put this victorious lifestyle in such vivid light it could be preached and demonstrated to the nations of the world. This is what Paul means when he says the mystery was "hidden for long ages past, but is now revealed." It was experienced before; but now it was explained by the coming of Jesus.

The second thing Paul says is that it was "made known through the prophetic writings by the command of the eternal God." This is a reference to the New Testament as we have it today. The apostles and prophets wrote the gospel down for us so we might have a clear picture of who Jesus is, and what he can be in us. This is why we must study the New Testament particularly (and the Old Testament as well), so we can understand how to live on the basis of the mystery.

Now Paul closes with a great doxology.

To the only wise God be glory forever through Jesus Christ! Amen.

What a plan! What a program! Let us renew our commitment to fulfill this mystery in every situation we face in life. Every moment of pressure and every demand upon us is simply an opportunity to realize again the validity of the mystery:

Christ in you, the hope of glory!